INTRODUCING
SCRIPTURE

ivp

INTRODUCING
SCRIPTURE

A GUIDE TO THE OLD & NEW TESTAMENTS

EDITED BY WAYNE GRUDEM,
C. JOHN COLLINS AND
THOMAS R. SCHREINER

INTER-VARSITY PRESS
Norton Street, Nottingham NG7 3HR, England
Email: ivp@ivpbooks.com
Website: www.ivpbooks.com

First published 2012

British Library Cataloguing in Publication Data
A catalogue record for this book is available from the British Library.

ISBN: 978–1–84474–568–5

Typeset in the United States of America
Printed and bound in Great Britain by Ashford Colour Press Ltd, Gosport,
Hampshire

Inter-Varsity Press publishes Christian books that are true to the Bible and
that communicate the gospel, develop discipleship and strengthen the
church for its mission in the world.

Inter-Varsity Press is closely linked with the Universities and Colleges
Christian Fellowship, a student movement connecting Christian Unions
in universities and colleges throughout Great Britain, and a member
movement of the International Fellowship of Evangelical Students.
Website: www.uccf.org.uk

Contents

CONTENTS

An Overview of the Bible's Storyline

Vern S. Poythress

How does the Bible as a whole fit together? The events recorded in the Bible took place over a span of thousands of years and in several different cultural settings. What is their unifying thread?

One unifying thread in the Bible is its divine authorship. *Every book of the Bible is God's word.* The events recorded in the Bible are there because God wanted them recorded, and he had them recorded with his people and their instruction in mind: "For whatever was written in former days was written for our instruction, that through endurance and through the encouragement of the Scriptures we might have hope" (Rom. 15:4).

God's Plan for History

The Bible also makes it clear that *God has a unified plan for all of history.* His ultimate purpose, "a plan for the fullness of time," is

7

"to unite all things in him [Christ], things in heaven and things on earth" (Eph. 1:10), "to the praise of his glory" (Eph. 1:12). God had this plan even from the beginning: "Remember the former things of old; for I am God, and there is no other; I am God, and there is none like me, declaring the end from the beginning and from ancient times things not yet done, saying, 'My counsel shall stand, and I will accomplish all my purpose' " (Isa. 46:9–10). "When the fullness of time had come," when the moment was appropriate in God's plan, "God sent forth his Son, born of woman, born under the law, to redeem those who were under the law" (Gal. 4:4–5).

The work of Christ on earth, and especially his crucifixion and resurrection, is the climax of history; it is the great turning point at which God actually accomplished the salvation toward which history had been moving throughout the Old Testament. The present era looks back on Christ's completed work but also looks forward to the consummation of his work when Christ will come again and when there will appear "new heavens and a new earth in which righteousness dwells" (2 Pet. 3:13; see Rev. 21:1–22:5).

The unity of God's plan makes it appropriate for him to include *promises and predictions* at earlier points in time, and then for the *fulfillments* of these to come at later points. Sometimes the promises take *explicit* form, as when God promises the coming of the Messiah, the great Savior whom Israel expected (Isa. 9:6–7). Sometimes the promises take *symbolic* form, as when God commanded animal sacrifices to be offered as a symbol for the forgiveness of sins (Leviticus 4). In themselves, the animal sacrifices were not able to remove sins permanently and to atone for them permanently (Heb. 10:1–18). They pointed forward to Christ, who is the final and complete sacrifice for sins.

Christ in the Old Testament

Since God's plan focuses on Christ and his glory (Eph. 1:10–12), it is natural that the promises of God and the symbols in the

Old Testament all point forward to him. "For all the promises of God find their Yes in him [Christ]" (2 Cor. 1:20). When Christ appeared to the disciples after his resurrection, his teaching focused on showing them how the Old Testament pointed to him: "And he said to them, 'O foolish ones, and slow of heart to believe all that the prophets have spoken! Was it not necessary that the Christ should suffer these things and enter into his glory?' And beginning with Moses and all the Prophets, he interpreted to them in all the Scriptures the things concerning himself" (Luke 24:25–27). One could also look at Luke 24:44–48: "Then he said to them, 'These are my words that I spoke to you while I was still with you, that everything written about me in the Law of Moses and the Prophets and the Psalms must be fulfilled.' Then he opened their minds to understand the Scriptures, and said to them, 'Thus it is written, that the Christ should suffer and on the third day rise from the dead, and that repentance and forgiveness of sins should be proclaimed in his name to all nations, beginning from Jerusalem. You are witnesses of these things.' "

When the Bible says that "he opened their minds to understand *the Scriptures*" (Luke 24:45), it cannot mean just a few scattered predictions about the Messiah. It means the Old Testament as a whole, encompassing all three of the major divisions of the Old Testament that the Jews traditionally recognized. "The Law of Moses" includes Genesis to Deuteronomy. "The Prophets" include both the "former prophets" (the historical books Joshua, Judges, 1–2 Samuel, and 1–2 Kings) and the "latter prophets" (Isaiah, Jeremiah, Ezekiel, and the Twelve Minor Prophets, Hosea–Malachi). "The Psalms" is representative of the third grouping by the Jews, called the "Writings." (The book of Daniel was placed in this group.) At the heart of understanding all these Old Testament books is the truth that they point forward to the suffering of Christ, his resurrection, and the subsequent spread of the gospel to "all nations" (Luke 24:47). The Old Testament as a whole, through its promises, its symbols, and its pictures of salvation, looks forward to the actual accomplishment of salvation that took place once for all in the life, death, and resurrection of Jesus Christ.

The Promises of God

In what ways does the Old Testament look forward to Christ? First, it directly points forward through *promises of salvation and promises concerning God's commitment to his people*. God gave some specific promises in the Old Testament relating to the coming of Christ as the Messiah, the Savior in the line of David. Through the prophet Micah, God promises that the Messiah is to be born in Bethlehem, the city of David (Mic. 5:2), a prophecy strikingly fulfilled in the New Testament (Matt. 2:1–12). But God often gives more general promises concerning a future great day of salvation, without spelling out all the details of how he will accomplish it (e.g., Isa. 25:6–9; 60:1–7). Sometimes he promises simply to be their God (see Gen. 17:7).

One common refrain is that, "I will be their God, and they shall be my people" (Jer. 31:33; see also Hos. 2:23; Zech. 8:8; 13:9; Heb. 8:10). Variations on this broad theme may sometimes focus more on the people and what they will be, while at other times they focus on God and what he will do. God's promise to "be their God" is really his comprehensive commitment to be with his people, to care for them, to discipline them, to protect them, to supply their needs, and to have a personal relationship with them. If that commitment continues, it promises to result ultimately in the final salvation that God works out in Christ.

The principle extends to all the promises in the Old Testament. "For all the promises of God find their Yes in him [Christ]" (2 Cor. 1:20). Sometimes God gives immediate, temporal blessings. These blessings are only a foretaste of the rich, eternal blessings that come through Christ: "Blessed be the God and Father of our Lord

Jesus Christ, who has blessed us in Christ with every spiritual blessing in the heavenly places" (Eph. 1:3).

Warnings and Curses

God's relation to people includes not only blessings but also warnings, threatenings, and cursings. These are appropriate because of God's righteous reaction to sin. They anticipate and point forward to Christ in two distinct ways. First, *Christ is the Lamb of God, the sin-bearer* (John 1:29; 1 Pet. 2:24). He was innocent of sin, but became sin for us and bore the curse of God on the cross (2 Cor. 5:21; Gal. 3:13). Every instance of the wrath of God against sin, and his punishments of sin, looks forward to the wrath that was poured out on Christ on the cross.

Second, *Christ at his second coming wars against sin and exterminates it.* The second coming and the consummation are the time when the final judgment against sin is executed. All earlier judgments against sin anticipate the final judgment. Christ during his earthly life anticipated this final judgment when he cast out demons and when he denounced the sins of the religious leaders.

Covenants

The promises of God in the Old Testament come in the context not only of God's commitment to his people but also of instruction about the people's commitment and obligations to God. Noah, Abraham, and others whom God meets and addresses are called on to respond not only with trust in God's promises but with lives that begin to bear fruit from their fellowship with God. The relation of God to his people is summed up in various *covenants* that God makes with people. A covenant between two human beings is a binding commitment obliging them to deal faithfully with one another (as with Jacob and Laban in Gen. 31:44). When God makes a covenant with man,

God is the sovereign, so he specifies the obligations on both sides. "I will be their God" is the fundamental obligation on God's side, while "they shall be my people" is the fundamental obligation on the human side. But then there are variations in the details.

For example, when God first calls Abram, he says, "Go from your country and your kindred and your father's house to the land that I will show you" (Gen. 12:1). This commandment specifies an obligation on the part of Abram, an obligation on the human side. God also indicates what he will do on his part: "And I will make of you a great nation, and I will bless you and make your name great, so that you will be a blessing" (Gen. 12:2). God's commitment takes the form of promises, blessings, and curses. The *promises and blessings* point forward to Christ, who is the fulfillment of the promises and the source of final blessings. The *curses* point forward to Christ both in his bearing the curse and in his execution of judgment and curse against sin, especially at the second coming.

The obligations on the human side of the covenants are also related to Christ. Christ is fully man as well as fully God. As a man, he stands with his people on the human side. He fulfilled the obligations of God's covenants through his perfect obedience (Heb. 5:8). He received the reward of obedience in his resurrection and ascension (see Phil. 2:9–10). The Old Testament covenants on their human side thus point forward to Christ's achievement.

By dealing with the wrath of God against sin, Christ changed a situation of alienation from God to a situation of peace. He reconciled believers to God (2 Cor. 5:18–21; Rom. 5:6–11). He brought personal intimacy with God, and the privilege of being children of God (Rom. 8:14–17). This intimacy is what all the Old Testament covenants anticipated. In Isaiah, God even declares that his servant, the Messiah, will be the covenant for the people (see Isa. 42:6; 49:8).

12

Offspring

It is worthwhile to focus on one specific element in Old Testament covenants, namely, the promise concerning offspring. In making a covenant with Abram, God calls on him to "walk before me, and be blameless" (Gen. 17:1). That is a human obligation in the covenant. On the divine side, God promises that he will make Abram "the father of a multitude of nations" (Gen. 17:4), and he renames him Abraham (Gen. 17:5). The covenant with Abraham in fact extends beyond Abraham to his posterity: "And I will establish my covenant between me and you and *your offspring after you* throughout their generations for an *everlasting* covenant, to be God to you and to your offspring after you. And I will give to you and to your offspring after you the land of your sojournings, all the land of Canaan, for an everlasting possession, and I will be their God" (Gen. 17:7–8).

The promises made to Abraham are exceedingly important within the Old Testament because they are the foundation for the nation of Israel. The history after Abraham shows that Abraham had a son, Isaac, in fulfillment of God's promise to Sarah. Isaac was the immediate result of God's promise of offspring who will inherit the land. Isaac in turn had a son, Jacob, and Jacob was the father of twelve sons who in turn multiplied into the twelve tribes of Israel. The nation of Israel became the next stage in the offspring that God promised.

But how does this relate to Christ? Christ is the descendant of David and of Abraham, as the genealogy in Matthew indicates (Matt. 1:1). Christ is the offspring of Abraham. In fact, he is the offspring in a uniquely emphatic sense: "Now the promises were made to Abraham and to his offspring. It does not say, 'And to offsprings,' referring to many, but referring to one, 'And to your offspring,' *who is Christ*" (Gal. 3:16; see Gen. 22:15–18).

Abraham was told to "walk before me, and be blameless" (Gen. 17:1). Abraham was basically a man of faith who trusted

God (Gal. 3:9; Heb. 11:8–12, 17–19). But Abraham also had his failures and sins. Who will walk before God and be blameless in an ultimate way? Not Abraham. Not anyone else on earth either, except Christ himself (Heb. 4:15). All the other candidates for being "offspring" of Abraham ultimately fail to be blameless. Thus the covenant with Abraham has an unbreakable tie to Christ. Christ is the ultimate offspring to whom the other offspring all point. One may go down the list of offspring: Isaac, Jacob, then the sons of Jacob. Among these sons, Judah is their leader who will have kingship (Gen. 49:10). David is the descendant of Abraham and Judah; Solomon is the descendant of David; and then comes Rehoboam and the others who descend from David and Solomon (Matt. 1:1–16).

Christ is not only the descendant of all of them by legal right; he is also superior to all of them as the uniquely blameless offspring. Through Christ believers are united to him and thereby themselves become "Abraham's offspring" (Gal. 3:29). Believers, Jews and Gentiles alike, become heirs to the promises of God made to Abraham and his offspring: "There is neither Jew nor Greek, there is neither slave nor free, there is no male and female, for you are all one in Christ Jesus. And if you are Christ's, then you are Abraham's offspring, heirs according to promise" (Gal. 3:28–29).

Christ as the Last Adam

Christ is not only the offspring of Abraham, but—reaching back farther in time to an earlier promise of God—the offspring of the woman: "I will put enmity between you [the serpent] and the woman, and between your offspring and her *offspring*; he shall bruise your head, and you shall bruise his heel" (Gen. 3:15). The conquest over the serpent, and therefore the conquest of evil and the reversal of its effects, is to take place through the offspring of the woman. One can trace this offspring down from Eve through Seth and his godly descendants, through Noah,

14

and down to Abraham, where God's promise takes the specific form of offspring for Abraham (see Luke 3:23–38, which traces Jesus's genealogy all the way back to Adam). Thus Christ is not only the offspring of Abraham but also the last Adam (1 Cor. 15:45–49). Like Adam, he represents all who belong to him. And he reverses the effects of Adam's fall.

Shadows, Prefigures, and "Types"

The New Testament constantly talks about Christ and the salvation that he has brought. That is obvious. What is not so obvious is that the same is true of the Old Testament, though it does this by way of *anticipation*. It gives us "shadows" and "types" of the things that were to come (see 1 Cor. 10:6, 11; Heb. 8:5).

For example, 1 Corinthians 10:6 indicates that the events the Israelites experienced in the wilderness were "examples for us." And 1 Corinthians 10:11 says, "Now these things happened to them as an example, but they were written down for our instruction, on whom the end of the ages has come." In 1 Corinthians 10:6 and 11, the Greek word for "example" is *typos*, from which derives the English word "type" (see Rom. 5:14).

A "type," in the language of theology, is *a special example, symbol, or picture that God designed beforehand, and that he placed in history at an earlier point in time in order to point forward to a later, larger fulfillment*. Animal sacrifices in the Old Testament prefigure the final sacrifice of Christ. So these animal sacrifices were "types" of Christ. The temple, as a dwelling place for God, prefigured Christ, who is the final "dwelling place" of God, and through whom God comes to be with his people (Matt. 1:23; John 2:21). The Old Testament priests were types of Christ, who is the final high priest (Heb. 7:11–8:7).

Fulfillment takes place preeminently in Christ (Eph. 1:10; 2 Cor. 1:20). But in the New Testament those people who are "in Christ," who place their trust in him and experience fellowship with his person and his blessings, receive the benefits of what he has accomplished, and therefore one can also find anticipations or "types" in the Old Testament that point forward to the New Testament church, the people in the New Testament who belong to Christ. For example, the Old Testament temple not only prefigured Christ, whose body is the temple (John 2:21), but prefigured the church, which is also called a temple (1 Cor. 3:16–17), because it is indwelt by the Holy Spirit. Some Old Testament symbols also may point forward especially to the consummation of salvation that takes place in the new heaven and the new earth yet to come (2 Pet. 3:13; Rev. 21:1–22:5). Old Testament Jerusalem prefigured the New Jerusalem that will come "down out of heaven from God" (Rev. 21:2).

Christ the Mediator

The Bible makes it clear that ever since the fall of Adam into sin, sin and its consequences have been the pervasive problem of the human race. It is a constant theme running through the Bible. Sin is rebellion against God, and it deserves death: "The wages of sin is death" (Rom. 6:23). God is holy, and no sinful human being, not even a great man like Moses, can stand in the presence of God without dying: "You cannot see my face, for man shall not see me and live" (Ex. 33:20). Sinful man needs a *mediator* who will approach God on his behalf. Christ, who is both God and man, and who is innocent of sin, is the only one who can serve: "There is one mediator between God and men, the man Christ Jesus, who gave himself as a ransom for all" (1 Tim. 2:5–6).

Though there is only one mediator in an ultimate sense, in a subordinate way various people in the Old Testament serve in some kind of mediatorial capacity. Moses is one of them. He went up to Mount Sinai to meet God while all the people waited at the bottom of the mountain (Exodus 19). When the people of Israel were terrified at hearing God's audible voice from the mountain, they asked for Moses to bring them God's words from then on (Ex. 20:18–21). God approved of the arrangement involving Moses bringing his words to the people (Deut. 5:28–33).

But if there is only one mediator, as 1 Timothy 2:5 says, how could Moses possibly serve in that way? Moses was not the ultimate mediator, but he *prefigured* Christ's mediation. Because Moses was sinful, he could not possibly have survived the presence of God without forgiveness, that is, without having a sinless mediator on his own behalf. God welcomed Moses into his presence only because, according to the plan of God, Christ was to come and make atonement for Moses. The benefits of Christ's work were reckoned beforehand for Moses's benefit. And so it must have been for all the Old Testament saints. How could they have been saved otherwise? God is perfectly holy, and they all needed perfection. Perfection was graciously reckoned to them because of Christ, who was to come.

That means that *there is only one way of salvation*, throughout the Old Testament as well as in the New Testament. Only Christ can save us. "And there is salvation in no one else, for there is no other name under heaven given among men by which we must be saved" (Acts 4:12). The instances of salvation in the Old Testament all depend on Christ. And in the Old Testament, salvation frequently comes through a *mediator*, a person or institution that stands between God and man. All the small instances of mediation in the Old Testament prefigure Christ. How else could it be, since there is only one mediator and one way of salvation?

So understanding of the unity of the Bible increases when one pays attention to *instances where God brings salvation, and instances where a mediator stands between God and man*. These instances include not only cases where God brings *spiritual* salvation in the form of personal fellowship, spiritual intimacy, and the promise of eternal life with God. They also include instances of *temporal*, external deliverance—"salvation" in a physical sense, which prefigures salvation in a spiritual sense. And indeed, salvation is not *merely* spiritual. Christians look forward to the resurrection of the body and to "new heavens and a new earth in which righteousness dwells" (2 Pet. 3:13). Personal salvation starts with renewal of the heart, but in the end it will be comprehensive and cosmic in scope. The Old Testament, when it pays attention to physical land and physical prosperity and physical health, anticipates the physicality of the believer's prosperity in the new heavens and the new earth.

Instances of mediators in the Old Testament include prophets, kings, and priests. *Prophets* bring the word of God from God to the people. *Kings*, when they submit to God, bring God's rule to bear on the people. *Priests* represent the people in coming before God's presence. Christ is the final prophet, king, and priest who fulfills all three functions in a final way (Heb. 1:1–3). One can also look at *wise men*, who bring God's wisdom to others; *warriors*, who bring God's deliverance from enemies; and singers, who bring praise to God on behalf of the people and speak of the character of God to the *people*.

Mediation occurs not only through human figures, but through institutions. *Covenants* play a mediatorial role in bringing God's word to the people. The *temple* brings God's presence to the people. The *animal sacrifices* bring God's forgiveness to the people. In reading the Bible one should look for ways in which God brings his word and his presence to people through *means* that he establishes. All these means perform a kind of mediatorial role, and because there is only one mediator, it is clear that they all point to Christ.

PART 1

OLD TESTAMENT

The Theology of the Old Testament

C. John Collins

When it comes to describing "the theology of the Old Testament," not everyone is convinced that there is a single theology represented in these diverse books. Many scholars have, however, tried to find a point of unity for all the books, often by proposing a single unifying theme, such as *covenant, or the kingdom of God, or the Messiah, or God himself.* These proposals do provide genuine insights, but they are often too oversimplified to do justice to the variety of materials in the Old Testament.

It will be more fruitful to understand the Old Testament as a whole in terms of an unfolding story, with a number of basic components: *monotheism, creation and fall, election and covenant, covenant membership,* and *eschatology.* This chapter will first explain these components, so that we can summarize the overarching story. Then we will consider briefly how the various parts of the Old Testament relate to this unfolding story, and consider how this provides a link to the New Testament authors' stance toward the Old Testament. The goal is to articulate some of the beliefs that will enable careful readers to profit more fully from reading the Old Testament books themselves.

The Components of the Story

1. *Monotheism.* There is only one true God, who made heaven and earth and all mankind. He made a material world that he is happy with, and he made it a fit place for human beings to live, and love, and serve. Every human being needs to know and love this God, whose spotless moral purity, magnificent power and wisdom, steadfast faithfulness, and unceasing love are breathtakingly beautiful. This one God rules over all things, and he will vindicate his own goodness and justice (in his own time). In ruling, God has not limited himself to working within the natural properties of what he has made, for he can go (and has gone) beyond these properties to do mighty deeds both in creation and in caring for his people.

The Old Testament invites Israel not simply to acknowledge the existence of this one true God, but to commit themselves to him in exclusive loyalty and love, centering their lives on the inestimable privilege of knowing him (Deut. 6:4–9). The fundamental character of this God is explained in Exodus 34:6–7, which focuses on his steadfast love and mercy (a passage frequently echoed in the rest of the Old Testament). The Old Testament also affirms that God is "righteous," that is, morally pure and perfect. Although this righteousness certainly results in God's work of punishing evildoers and vindicating his own moral character, the term commonly emphasizes God's reliability in keeping his promises (e.g., Pss. 71:2; 116:5).

The Old Testament does not explicitly describe God as a trinity. Rather, with its references to God's Spirit (e.g., Gen. 1:2), its use of "us/our" for God (e.g., Gen. 1:26), and its indications or hints of a divine Messiah (e.g., Ps. 110:5; Isa. 9:6; see Ezek. 34:15, 23), it lays the groundwork for the fuller declaration of divine triunity that is found in the New Testament (Matt. 28:19; 1 Cor. 12:4–6; 2 Cor. 13:14).

2. *Creation and fall.* The one Creator God made the first human beings, Adam and Eve, with dignity and purpose; their calling was to live faithfully to God and to spread the blessings of Eden throughout the earth. Because Adam and Eve betrayed God's purpose, all people since the fall are beset with sins and weaknesses that only God's grace can redeem and heal.

3. *Election and covenant.* The one true God chose a people for himself and bound himself to them by his covenant (Ex. 19:4–6; Deut. 7:6–11). This covenant expressed God's intention to save the people, and through them to bring light to the rest of the world, in order to restore all things to their proper functioning in the world God made. The land of Israel was to be a kind of reconstituted Eden, which would flourish as the people's faithfulness flourished (or languish if the people were unfaithful). God's covenants generally involve one person who represents the whole people (e.g., Adam, Noah, Abraham, David); the rest of the people experience the covenant by virtue of their inclusion in the community represented. The representative is required to embody the ideal of covenant faithfulness as a model for those on whose behalf he has acted.

4. *Covenant membership.* In his covenant, God offers his grace to his people: the forgiveness of their sins, the shaping of their lives in this world to reflect his own glory, and a part to play in bringing light to the Gentiles. Each member of God's people is responsible to lay hold of this grace from the heart: to believe the promises (see Paul's use of Abraham and David as examples of faith in Rom. 4:1–25; see also Heb. 11:1–40), and then to grow in obeying the commands, and to keep on doing so all their lives long. Those who lay hold in this way are the faithful.

23

These people, as distinct from the unfaithful among them, enjoy the full benefits of God's love. Each Israelite is a member of a people, a corporate entity; the members have a mutual participation in the life of the people as a whole. Thus the spiritual and moral well-being of the whole affects the well-being of each of the members, and each member contributes to the others by his own spiritual and moral life. Thus each one shares the joys and sorrows of the others, and of the whole. Historical judgments upon the whole people often come because too many of the members are unfaithful; these judgments do not, however, bring the story of God's people to an end but serve rather to purify and chasten that people (often by removing unbelieving members).

It is important for Christian readers to sharpen their grasp of how the Old Testament uses words such as "salvation" and "judgment." When the Old Testament speaks of God "redeeming" his people (e.g., Ex. 15:13) or "saving" them (e.g., Ex. 14:30), it refers to God's gracious dealings for the sake of this corporate entity, the people: he calls it, he protects it, he purifies it, in order to foster the conditions under which the life of its members may flourish. The Old Testament can also speak of God giving "salvation" or "redemption" to particular persons (e.g., Pss. 3:2, 7; 19:14). Generally in the Old Testament, however, such expressions refer to members of the people experiencing the benefits of covenant membership, whether that be forgiveness of sins, or deliverance from some trouble or persecution, or something else—tracing everything back to the grace of God that led him to make the covenant originally and now to keep it in effect. When Christians speak of personal salvation, they usually are thinking of individuals in isolation, and so have a much narrower meaning in mind; they should consider whether the New Testament usage is closer to the Old Testament usage than they might have realized hitherto, including both every aspect of their lives and their connections to other believers, and thus extending to a wider range of experience than simply their souls.

The "law," given through Moses, plays a vital role in the Old Testament. It is uniformly presented as an object of delight and admiration (e.g., Psalm 119), because it is a gift from a loving and gracious God. The law is never presented in the Old Testament as a list of rules that one must obey in order to be right with God; rather, it is God's fatherly instruction, given to shape the people he has loved and saved into a community of faith, holiness, and love, bound together by mutual support and care. The various laws, with their penalties for infractions and provisions for repayment, were designed to protect that community from the failures of its members, and the moral guidelines gave specific form to what the restored image of God would look like in the agrarian culture of ancient Israel. Right at the heart of this system is worship at the sanctuary, with its provisions for atonement and forgiveness for those who have gone astray. Sadly, only in a very few instances in the Old Testament do we see anything that even remotely matches this ideal, whether on a large scale (Josh. 22:1–34 is an excellent example, distinctive for its rarity) or on a small one (e.g., Boaz in the book of Ruth, who embodies the Lord's own kindness to a foreign-born "proselyte"). The prophets anticipated an era, after Judah's return from exile in Babylon, in which God's people would really take the law into their own hearts (e.g., Ezek. 36:25–27); the covenant renewal that the postexilic community experienced was, however, only a brief foretaste of that expectation. (Interpreters debate the way in which this relates to the spread of Christianity among the Gentiles—is it focused primarily on *Israel* laying hold of the covenant properly, or does it describe the new arrangement that Jesus's resurrection brought in?—but that is outside the scope of this chapter.)

5. *Eschatology.* The story of God's people is headed toward a glorious future in which all kinds of people will come to know

the Lord and join his people. This was the purpose for which God called Abraham (Gen. 12:1–3), and for which he appointed Israel (Ex. 19:4–6). It is part of the dignity of God's people that, in God's mysterious wisdom, their personal faithfulness contributes to the story getting to its goal (see Deut. 4:6–8).

The Old Testament develops its idea of a Messiah (eventually clarified as the ultimate heir of David) in the light of these components. The earliest strands of the messianic idea speak of an offspring who will undo the work of the Evil One and bless the Gentiles by bringing them into his kingdom (Gen. 3:15; 22:17–18; 24:60); the idea that kings will descend from Abraham (Gen. 17:6, 16) and Jacob (Gen. 35:11) becomes focused on the tribe of Judah, to which the obedience of the peoples will be brought (Gen. 49:10). The kings in David's line carry this idea forward. They are to embody the people: just as the people as a whole is God's son (Ex. 4:22–23), so also the Davidic king is God's son (2 Sam. 7:14; Ps. 89:26–27). The promise of a lasting dynasty for David (2 Sam. 7:16) becomes the expectation that a final heir of his line will one day arise, take his Davidic throne (in "the last days"), and lead his people in the great task of bringing light to the Gentiles (e.g., Pss. 2:8; 72:8–11, 17 [using Gen. 22:18]; Isa. 9:6–7; 11:1–10; see Isa. 42:1–9).

The Parts of the Old Testament in Relation to the Story

The Old Testament is thus the story of the one true Creator God, who called the family of Abraham to be his remedy for the defilement that came into the world through the sin of Adam and Eve. God rescued Israel from slavery in Egypt in fulfillment of this plan, and established them as a theocracy for the sake of displaying his existence and character to the rest of the world. God sent his blessings and curses upon Israel in order to pursue that purpose. God never desisted from that purpose, even in the face of the most grievous unfaithfulness in Israel.

This overarching story serves as a grand narrative or worldview story for Israel: each member of the people was to see himself or herself as an *heir* of this story, with all its glory and shame; as a *steward* of the story, responsible to pass it on to the next generation; and as a *participant*, whose faithfulness could play a role, by God's mysterious wisdom, in the story's progress.

Some who have seen this category of Israel's story as a key to Old Testament theology have argued for reading the entire Old Testament *as a story*. This does not help the reader, for the very obvious reason that not everything in the Old Testament is narrative or "story." For example, there are *laws* (in the Pentateuch), whose purpose was to protect equity and civility in the theocracy by guiding judges in what penalties to impose and by specifying the minimum standard of behavior necessary to preserve the theocracy (many of the specific laws do not intend to spell out the moral ideal for the members of Israel, which comes from likeness to God in the creation account and from the goal of community holiness; the "perfection" of the laws consist in the way they serve the social fabric of God's people); there is *wisdom* (in the books of Job, Proverbs, and Ecclesiastes, as well as in the Psalms), which helps the members to live well daily; there are *songs* (esp. the Psalms) that the people of God should sing in corporate worship; there are *poems* (esp. the Song of Solomon; see Prov. 5:15–20) celebrating such wonders as romantic love; and lots more. Therefore it is better to speak of reading the parts of the Old Testament *in relation* to its overarching story. That is, we can see the parts in relation to the Big Story that unifies the whole. The Proverbs help people to live their little stories in such a way as to contribute to the Big Story. The Psalms—many of which explicitly recount parts of the Big Story—help people live as faithful members of the worshiping corporate entity, the people of God. The Prophets keep recalling the Big Story, the direction in which Israel's story is headed, calling their audiences

27

to live faithfully in its light. The Big Story tells us that God's purpose is to restore our humanity to its proper function, and thus it reminds each person of the human nature he shares with every other human being, and of the duty and benefit of seeking the good of others. For example, enjoying the love of a faithful spouse is a way of experiencing renewed humanity—a way that displays God's goodness to the rest of the world (as in the Song of Solomon).

All of these factors explain why it is possible for the New Testament authors both to say that the Sinai covenant is done away with (see below), because it was focused on the theocracy, which had an end in mind from the beginning (when the Gentiles would receive the light in large measure)—and at the same time to affirm that this covenant has embedded in it principles that cannot pass away, because they are part of the larger story of which the Sinai covenant is one chapter.

The Old Testament as Christian Scripture

The Old Testament presents itself, then, as a story that is headed somewhere. The Old Testament closes with both anxiety and hope under Persian rule (see Malachi). The books of the Second Temple period (between the Old and New Testaments) continue this notion of Israel as God's people chosen for a purpose, but not all strands of this material make clear what that purpose is. Some of these Second Temple books offer endings for the story (e.g., in the Qumran community as the elect); but the faithful were looking for more. (For more information on the Second Temple period, see ch. 6.) The New Testament authors, most of whom were *Jewish* Christians, saw themselves as heirs of the Old Testament story, and as authorized to describe its proper completion in the death and resurrection of Jesus and the messianic era that this ushered in. These authors appropriated the Old Testament as Christian Scripture, and they urged their audiences (many of whom were *Gentile* Christians) to do the same. There is debate over just how the New Testament authors used the Old Testament as Scripture, but the simplest summary of the New Testament authors' stance would be to say that they saw the Old Testament as constituting the earlier chapters of the story in which Christians are now participating.

This construct, of earlier and later chapters in the story of God's work for his people, allows us to understand how the Old Testament era and the Christian era will have elements both of continuity and of discontinuity. The Old Testament had looked forward to an internationalized people of God, without explaining exactly how that would connect to the theocracy of Israel (see Ps. 87:4–6). The theocracy defined the people of God as predominantly coming from a particular ethnic group in a particular land; Gentile converts ("sojourners") were protected (Ex. 12:49; 20:10; 22:21; Lev. 19:10) but could not be full-status members of the theocratic community (see Deut. 14:21; 15:3. Num. 34:14–15 shows that land was allocated to Israelites alone). The New Testament abolishes the distinction (Eph. 2:19), because the theocracy as such is no longer in existence and many of its provisions are done away with (see Acts 10:34–35; Heb. 9:11–14). At the same time, the character of the one Creator God, and his interest in restoring the image of God in human beings, transcends the specific arrangements of the theocracy; hence, the moral commands of God apply to Christians as they did to the faithful in Israel (see Rom. 13:8–10).

2

Introduction to the Pentateuch

Gordon Wenham

The Name of the Pentateuch

The Pentateuch (Gk. "five-volumed") consists of the first five books of the Bible, Genesis through Deuteronomy. The Hebrew term for it is *torah* ("law" or "instruction"), so this is how the New Testament refers to it (Gk. *nomos*, "law"). In the Hebrew Bible, the law is the first of the three major sections, and sometimes *nomos* may refer to the whole Old Testament (e.g., John 10:34). Although the Pentateuch contains many laws, it is essentially narrative with episodes of law-giving, but in the broader sense of *torah* all the Pentateuch can be seen as instruction, for it teaches as much through the history it records as by the law it gives. Another name for the Pentateuch found in some translations is "the five books of Moses." This is also an apt description in that the books of Exodus to Deuteronomy provide a biography of Moses, and traditionally he has been seen as their main author.

The Pentateuch as Foundational to the Whole Bible

The Pentateuch is not simply the beginning of the Bible; it is also the foundation of the Bible. It serves to orient the reader for reading the rest of the biblical story line. It introduces the key promises that show God's purposes in history and that lay the groundwork for the coming of Christ. Its theological ideas and ethical principles inform the rest of the Bible so that the subsequent books assume its authority and appeal to it as they evaluate people's deeds and character. These points are illustrated briefly here:

1. *Orientation.* The beginning of a book sets its tone and gives clues to the author's perspective. Genesis did this for the ancient world of polytheism by explaining that the world is created and controlled by only one God, not by a crowd of competing gods and goddesses. Similarly it speaks to today's readers, who often are essentially atheists (whether consciously or unconsciously): it shows them what it means to believe that behind all the phenomena of nature and the laws of science there is an all-powerful, loving God who controls all that happens.

2. *Divine purposes.* The Pentateuch shows God's intentions for his creation by describing what the world was like when he first created man and woman in the garden of Eden. Their sin sets back the divine program but does not defeat it, for God later calls Abraham and promises him descendants, land, and, most important of all, blessing through his descendants to all the nations. These promises are more fully developed in the later books of the Pentateuch.

3. *Theology and ethics.* The Pentateuch gives insight into God's character and his ethical standards. It illustrates both his benevolence and his righteousness. He cares for mankind, creating man in his own image, providing him with food, and protecting human life from violent assault. Yet at the same time he demands moral behavior, from keeping the Sabbath to refusing

adultery or theft. Tales of punishment, from the flood (Genesis 6–9) to the golden calf (Exodus 32), demonstrate the danger of disregarding divine standards.

Content

A review of the contents of the Pentateuch shows that its center of gravity is *the law-giving at Sinai*. All of Exodus 19 to Numbers 10 is devoted to the events that occurred in the vicinity of Sinai: the declaration of the Ten Commandments, the building of the tabernacle, the laws governing sacrifice, entry to the tabernacle, and the celebration of the festivals. Closer examination of this central section suggests that its climax is *God's glory filling the newly built tabernacle* (Ex. 40:34–38) as a visible demonstration of his choice of and intimacy with Israel—a restoration of the situation in the garden of Eden, where God walked with Adam and Eve (Gen. 3:8).

But the outer frame of the books of Exodus to Deuteronomy is constituted by *the life of Moses*. Exodus 2 tells of his birth and providential upbringing in the Egyptian court, while Deuteronomy 34 describes his death. Exodus 3–15 describes his call to lead his people and the establishment of his authority over Pharaoh in the eyes of the Israelites (Ex. 14:31). Moses's approaching death colors all the final chapters of the Pentateuch. He is told to prepare for his death in Numbers 27, and the whole of Deuteronomy consists of his last appeals to the nation to serve the Lord faithfully. To this end he preaches three sermons and recites two poems (Deuteronomy 32–33) before he is granted a vision of the Promised Land and dies (Deuteronomy 34).

The book of Genesis serves as an introduction to the rest of the Pentateuch. It explains the context for Moses's life and ministry. It gives the origin of the nation of Israel and its tribes, and explains how they came to be living in Egypt though their ancestors had been promised the land of Canaan. The people of Israel are to bring blessing to the nations, and the opening chapters of Genesis show the desperate need of the nations for blessing. The first avalanche of sin led to the universal judgment of the flood. The new start with Noah and his sons was again derailed, first by the sin of Ham (Gen. 9:20–29) and then by the Tower of Babel (Gen. 11:1–9). In this general way Genesis explains the situation that Moses confronted, and various episodes in the lives of the patriarchs also show parallels to Moses's experience (for example, Abraham's exodus from Egypt in Gen. 12:10–20).

Time Span

It is striking that the earliest events in the Bible are dated more precisely than the later ones. For example, the different stages of the flood are dated to the exact day of the year (Gen. 7:11; 8:4–5). The ages of the pre-flood heroes at the fathering of their firstborn and at their death are carefully noted in Genesis 5. Taking these figures at face value, Archbishop Usher (1581–1656) calculated that the creation of the world occurred in 4004 BC. Using similar principles, Orthodox Jews hold that the year 2000 was the year 5760 (i.e., 5,760 years since creation).

Such a venerable interpretative approach cannot be glibly dismissed, but most conservative interpreters today believe that it does not account well enough for the literary conventions of Moses's day. For example, the genealogies do not claim to include every generation, and may skip any number of them. With respect to the long lives of the antediluvians (those who lived before the flood), some scholars think these numbers should be understood as their actual ages in years, while others think their ages expressed in multiple centuries may have a symbolic significance, in line with the practices of other ancient peoples. It is best to admit one's ignorance here; yet at least it can be said that Moses used these numbers to make a point about the antiquity and reality of his audience's forebears.

However, the dating of the Israelite patriarchs by the internal numbering system of the Old Testament is not so problematic. Conservative biblical scholars think it is likely that Abraham, Isaac, and Jacob lived in the late third and early second millennium BC, and that the Israelites entered Egypt either in the early nineteenth century BC (consistent with an early date for the exodus; see Ex. 12:40) or else in the seventeenth or sixteenth century BC, during the Egyptian Second Intermediate Period (1640–1532 BC). The Hyksos Dynasty that ruled during this time came from outside Egypt and therefore could have welcomed Hebrews like Joseph and his family to play a prominent part in Egyptian life.

The date of the exodus from Egypt is likewise controversial. Combining the biblical and extrabiblical evidence points to Solomon's temple being built in 967 or 966 BC. According to 1 Kings 6:1, Solomon began to build the temple 480 years after the exodus. If the author intended "480 years" as a literal designation, then working backward suggests the exodus would have been in 1447 or 1446 BC, which is the date preferred by many conservative Old Testament scholars today. However, on the basis of the description of the events surrounding the exodus (such as building the cities of Pithom and Raamses), most Egyptologists prefer a date in the 1200s—preferably after 1279 BC but certainly before 1209, when an Egyptian monument mentions that Israel was established as a people in the land of Canaan. If there is symbolism in the designation "480 years," then it is possible that the exodus took place in the early 1200s BC rather than in the mid-1400s.

Composition

For more than two thousand years, readers of the Pentateuch assumed that Moses was its author (see Mark 7:10). This was a natural conclusion to draw from its contents, for most of the laws are said to have been given to Moses by God (e.g., Lev. 1:1), and indeed some passages are explicitly said to have been written down by Moses (see Deut. 31:9, 24). The account of his death could have been recorded by someone else, though some held it was a prophetic account by Moses himself (Deuteronomy 34).

But in the late eighteenth century, critical scholars began challenging the assumption of Mosaic authorship. They argued that several authors were responsible for writing the Pentateuch. These authors supposedly wrote many centuries after Moses, and were separated from each other in time and location. Complicated theories were developed to explain how the Pentateuch grew as different authors' accounts were spliced and adjusted by a series of editors. According to these critical scholars, it was likely that the Pentateuch reached its final form in the fifth century BC, nearly a millennium after Moses.

In the late twentieth century this type of critical theory was strongly attacked, not just by conservative scholars but also by those brought up on such theories. They argue that the theories are too complicated, self-contradictory, and ultimately unprovable. It is much more rewarding and less speculative to focus interpretative effort on the final form of the text. So there is a strong move to abandon the compositional theories of the nineteenth and early twentieth centuries for simpler hypotheses. Thus some critical scholars would see the Pentateuch being an essentially fifth-century BC creation. Others suggest earlier dates. But none of these suggestions can really be proven.

The Pentateuch does undoubtedly claim to be divine in origin, mediated through Moses. Thus Moses should be looked to as the original human author. Indeed, as stated above, the Pentateuch looks like a life of Moses, with an introduction. But this need not mean that he wrote every word of the present Pentateuch. It seems likely that the spelling and the grammar of the Pentateuch were revised to keep it intelligible for later readers. Also, a number of features in the text look like clarifications for a later age. But this is quite different from supposing that the Pentateuch was essentially composed in a later age. Rather, it should be seen as originating in Moses's time but undergoing some slight revision in later eras so later readers could understand its message and apply it to their own situations.

Theme

The theme of the Pentateuch is announced in Genesis 12:1–3, the call of Abraham: "Go from your country . . . to the land that I will show you. And I will make of you a great nation, and I will bless you . . . and in you all the families of the earth shall be blessed." Here God promises Abraham four things: (1) a land to live in; (2) numerous descendants ("a great nation"); (3) blessing (divinely granted success) for himself; and (4) blessing through him for all the nations of the world. God's benefit for the nations is the climax or goal of the promises: the preceding promises of land, descendants, and personal blessing are steps on the way to the final goal of universal blessing.

Each time God appears to the patriarchs, the promises are elaborated and made more specific. For example, the promise of an unidentified "land" in Genesis 12:1 becomes "this land" in Genesis 12:7 and "all the land of Canaan, for an everlasting possession" in Genesis 17:8.

The fulfillment of these promises to Abraham constitutes the story line of the Pentateuch. It is a story of gradual and often difficult fulfillment. The birth of children to produce a great nation is no easy matter: the patriarchs' wives—Sarah, Rebekah, and Rachel—all have great trouble conceiving (Gen. 17:17; 25:21; 30:1). But by the time they enter Egypt, Jacob's family numbers seventy (Gen. 46:27; Ex. 1:5). After many years in Egypt they have become so numerous that the Egyptians perceive them as a threat (Ex. 1:7–10), and when the first census is taken, they total 603,550 fighting men (Num. 1:46).

Similarly the promise of land is very slow in being fulfilled. Abraham acquires a well at Beersheba, and a burial plot for Sarah at Hebron (Gen. 21:30–31; 23:1–20). Jacob bought some land near Shechem (Gen. 33:19), but then late in life he and the rest of the family emigrated to Egypt (Genesis 46–50). The book of Exodus begins with the hope of a quick return to Canaan, but the stubbornness of Pharaoh delays Israel's departure. Their journey through the Sinai wilderness is eventful, and after about a year they reach Kadesh on the very borders of Canaan. There, scared by the report of some of the spies, the people rebel against Moses and the God-given promises, so they are condemned to wander in the wilderness for forty years (Numbers 13–14). And of course the Pentateuch ends with Moses dying outside the Promised Land, and the people hoping to enter it.

For these reasons the theme of the Pentateuch has been described as the *partial* fulfillment of the promises to the patriarchs. Such a description certainly fits the climactic promise that through Abraham and his descendants all the families of the earth would be blessed. The closest fulfillment of this in the Pentateuch is Joseph saving Egypt and the surrounding lands from starvation in the seven-year famine. But later on, Israel is seen as a threat by other peoples in the region such as the Moabites, Midianites, and Amorites. It is not apparent how or when all the peoples of the world will be blessed. At the end of the Pentateuch that, like the promise of land, still awaits fulfillment.

But the promise of blessing to the patriarchs and their descendants is abundantly fulfilled within the Pentateuch—despite their frequent lack of faith and their willful rebellion. For example, after Abraham lied about his wife and allowed her to be taken by a foreign king, the pair escape, greatly enriched (Genesis 12; 20). Jacob, forced to flee from home after cheating his father, eventually returns with great flocks and herds to meet a forgiving brother (Genesis 27–33). The nation of Israel breaks the first two commandments by making the golden calf, yet enjoys the privilege of God dwelling among them in the tabernacle (Exodus 32–40). The Pentateuch is thus *a story of divine mercy to a wayward people.*

However, alongside this account of God's grace must be set *the importance of the law and right behavior.* The opening chapters of Genesis set out the pattern of life that everyone should follow: monogamy, Sabbath observance, rejection of personal vengeance and violence—principles that even foreigners living in ancient Israel were expected to observe. But Israel was chosen to mediate between God and the nations and to demonstrate in finer detail what God expected of human society, so that other peoples would exclaim, "What great nation has a god so near to it . . . ? And what great nation is there, that has statutes and rules so righteous as all this law . . . ?" (Deut. 4:7–8).

To encourage Israel's compliance with all the law revealed at Sinai, it was embedded in a covenant. This involved Israel giving its assent to the Ten Commandments and the other laws on worship, personal behavior, crime, and so on. Obedience to these laws guaranteed Israel's future blessing and prosperity, whereas disobedience would be punished by crop failure, infertility, loss of God's presence, defeat by enemies, and, eventually, exile to a foreign land (see Leviticus 26; Deuteronomy 28).

These covenantal principles—that *God will bless Israel when she keeps the law and punish her when she does not*—pervade the rest of the Old Testament. The book of Joshua demonstrates that fidelity to the law led to the successful conquest of the land, while the books of Judges and Kings show that Israel's apostasy to other gods led to defeat by her enemies. The argument of the prophets is essentially that Israel's failure to keep the law puts her at risk of experiencing the divine punishments set out in Leviticus 26 and Deuteronomy 28.

Since New Testament times, Christians have seen the promises in the Pentateuch as finding their ultimate fulfillment in Christ. Jesus is the offspring of the woman who bruises the serpent's head (Gen. 3:15). He is the one through whom "all the families of the earth shall be blessed" (Gen. 12:3). He is the star and scepter who shall rise out of Israel (Num. 24:17). More than this, many heroes of the Old Testament have been seen as types of Christ. Jesus is the second Adam. He is the true Israel (Jacob), whose life sums up the experience of the nation.

But preeminently Jesus is seen as the new and greater Moses. As Moses declared God's law for Israel, so Jesus declares and embodies God's word to the nations. As Moses suffered and died outside the land so that his people could enter it, so the Son of God died on earth so that his people might enter heaven. It was observed that the filling of the tabernacle with the glory of God was the climax of the Pentateuch (Ex. 40:34–38). So too "the Word became flesh and dwelt among us, and we have seen his glory" (John 1:14). The goal of the entire Bible is that humans everywhere should glorify the God whose glory has confronted them. Lost sight of in Eden, this goal reappears through Moses, on its way to final fulfillment through Christ.

3

Introduction to the Historical Books

David Howard

The "Historical Books" of the Old Testament, which come after the Pentateuch, tell the story of (1) Israel's entry into the Promised Land of Canaan under Joshua; (2) Israel's life in the land under the judges and the transition to kingship; (3) the division of the nation into two rival kingdoms (Israel and Judah) and life in both; (4) the downfall and exile of each kingdom; (5) life in the exile; and (6) Judah's return from exile. These books span close to one thousand years of history, so it is not surprising that their story includes many ups and downs, twists and turns. Yet, through it all, the God who is the same yesterday, today, and forever remains the focal point of all of these books.

The date of Moses's death is calculated by working backward from 1 Kings 6:1, which states that Solomon began to build the temple 480 years after the exodus from Egypt. Comparing the information in 1 Kings with extrabiblical records indicates that the

Fig. 3.1 Historical Books Timeline

1406 [or 1220] BC	Moses's death; Israel's entry into Canaan under Joshua
1375 [or 1210]	Joshua's death
1375–1055 [or 1210–1050/42/30]	Period of the judges
1050/42/30–1010	Saul's reign
1010–971	David's reign
971–931	Solomon's reign
931–722	Divided kingdom (Israel)—19 kings
722	Destruction of Samaria (Israel's capital) by Assyria; Israel's resettlement
931–586	Divided kingdom (Judah)—19 kings, 1 queen
586	Destruction of Jerusalem and temple by Babylon; Judah exiled to Babylon
586–538	Judah's exile in Babylon
561	Release of King Jehoiachin from prison in Babylon
539	Cyrus II of Persia captures Babylon
538	First return of Jews to Jerusalem under Jeshua and Zerubbabel
516	Temple rebuilding completed
478	Esther and Mordecai rise in the Persian court
458	Ezra's return to Jerusalem from Babylon
445	Nehemiah's return to Jerusalem from Babylon
445–???	Walls of Jerusalem rebuilt
433	Nehemiah's visit to Babylon and return to Jerusalem

temple building began in 967 or 966 BC. The date of the exodus, then, would be 1447 or 1446 BC, and the date of Moses's death, forty years later, would be 1407 or 1406. On the other hand, if one finds some symbolism in the 480-year figure (e.g., supposing it to result from twelve generations, with a generation taken to be forty years), one may arrive at a date for the exodus of about 1260 BC (which some believe allows for greater agreement with Egyptian history), yielding a date around 1220 for Moses's death.

Other dates are certain with a high degree of confidence. The story of Esther and Mordecai took place in the time of Ahasuerus (Est. 1:1), who reigned over Persia 486–464 BC

Note that the northern kingdom of Israel lasted slightly more than two hundred years (931–722 BC), with nineteen kings. All of Israel's kings did evil in the Lord's eyes, and there were several assassinations and changes of ruling family.

In contrast, the southern kingdom of Judah lasted almost 350 years (931–586 BC), with the same number of kings. Thus, a greater degree of political stability existed in Judah—and, to some degree, spiritual stability, since eight kings in Judah did right in the Lord's eyes. All the kings in this lineage were descended from David, to whom God had promised there would always be a descendant of his line on the throne (2 Sam. 7:12–16).

The Babylonians attacked Jerusalem in 605 and 597 BC, deporting the cream of Judah's society (e.g., Daniel and his friends were deported in 605) before the final destruction and deportation of 586.

From the dates above, it appears as though the exile lasted only fifty years (586–538/537 BC), which seems to contradict Jeremiah's prophecy about the return from exile after seventy years (Jer. 25:11; 29:10). However, the round number "70" can be calculated by one of two methods: (a) from the first deportation (605 BC) to the first return (538 or 537) yields sixty-eight years; or (b) from the destruction of Jerusalem and the temple (586) to the rebuilding of the temple (516) yields seventy years.

Unity

In our English Bibles, there are twelve Historical Books: Joshua, Judges, Ruth, 1–2 Samuel, 1–2 Kings, 1–2 Chronicles, Ezra, Nehemiah, and Esther. In the Hebrew Bible, the books are divided differently: Joshua, Judges, 1–2 Samuel, and 1–2 Kings are part of the second section of the Bible, titled the "Former Prophets," and the rest of the Historical Books are found among the third section, titled the "Writings."

Each book evidences a different style of writing. In Joshua, for example, the accounts of Israel's entering and settling into the land of Canaan in chapters 1–11 and 22–24 are interrupted by the lists of land distributions in chapters 12–21. In Judges, we find a cyclical history spiraling downward through the regimes of successive judges. Ruth is a self-contained and beautifully told story of God's grace in the life of one family of David's ancestors. First and 2 Samuel tell of the establishment of the legitimate Davidic monarchy in a richly textured account of the events; much in these books has the feel of an eyewitness account. By contrast, 1 and 2 Kings tell the story of Israel's kings after David in a much more stereotypical manner, structured around repeated formulas of the accession, main exploits, and deaths of the successive kings, all leading eventually to exile. First and 2 Chronicles portray similar events to those found in 2 Samuel and 1–2 Kings. As with the composition of Kings, Chronicles enlists and shapes an array of literary and historical materials to address a new set of concerns now facing the postexilic people of God. Ezra–Nehemiah contains first-person and eyewitness accounts, lists, and correspondence about the return from Babylonian exile and postexilic life. Esther is like Ruth in being a self-contained and well-told story; it deals with life events affecting Jews in Persia in the postexilic period.

Despite the differences, all of these books present history from a God's-eye view. That is, they are not "history for history's sake," but rather, they are *theological* in nature. They tell about God's repeated in-breakings into history, whether by dramatic accounts of miracles, or by God's speaking directly to his people, or by his indirect presence, visible in the providential outworking of events. And, in the telling of all these events, the authors' perspectives are God's perspectives. So it should not surprise us that many of the books' themes echo each other and also carry forward some of the great themes of the Pentateuch.

Themes

Each historical book has its own unique themes. But many of these can be tied into larger, overarching themes that have their roots in the Pentateuch and unfold across many books. Five over-arching themes pervade the Historical Books: God's sovereignty, presence, promises, kingdom, and covenant.

1. God's Sovereignty: Over Israel and the Nations

God is consistently presented in the Historical Books as sovereign over all of creation, including the elements of nature and the affairs of individuals and nations. The most spectacular way in which the writers demonstrate God's sovereignty is through various miracles. These occur throughout the Old Testament but tend to be especially prominent in the book of Joshua (the stopping of the Jordan River and various victories over enemies) and the books of 1–2 Kings, especially in the stories of Elijah and Elisha (1 Kings 17–19; 21; 2 Kings 1–9; 13).

Also, Israel is consistently presented as under God's authority, care, and protection, and therefore obligated to return to him their love, trust, and obedience. Even the other nations were subject to God—from the small city-states and peoples in the times of Joshua, the judges, Saul, and David (e.g., the Philistines, Moabites, Canaanites), to the great empires of Assyria, Babylon, and Persia. These circumstances form the backdrop to the events of 1–2 Kings, 1–2 Chronicles, Ezra–Nehemiah, and Esther.

2. God's Presence: Near and Far

In most of the Historical Books, God is close at hand. He designated Joshua as Moses's successor, raised up the judges in response to Israel's dire straits over several centuries, and designated Saul and then David as his chosen kings. He was a source of help to the godly kings who sought him, and to bold prophets who spoke in his name (Nathan, Gad, Elijah, Micaiah, Elisha, Huldah, and others). He empowered Jeshua, Zerubbabel, Ezra, and Nehemiah to be bold leaders after the trauma of the exile. The prayers of godly kings such as David (2 Samuel 7), Solomon

(1 Kings 8), Jehoshaphat (2 Chronicles 20), and others show the closeness of their relationship with God.

And yet at times God seemed more hidden. Most often, this was because of Israel's sin. Such was clearly the case in Judges (ch. 2), Samuel (1 Sam. 4:19–22), and repeatedly in 1–2 Kings and 1–2 Chronicles. Sometimes, however, God's hiddenness is not attributed to sin; it is simply a fact, and his presence must be inferred indirectly. In Ruth, for example, the author quotes the characters' references to God many times, but only mentions God in his own words twice (Ruth 1:6; 4:13). In Esther, God is not mentioned at all. Cases such as these (esp. Esther) signal that sometimes Christians have to look for God's presence in very intentional ways, and that sometimes God chooses not to reveal himself as directly as at other times.

3. God's Promises: Present and Future

The Historical Books carry forward the stories of the Pentateuch, including some of its great themes. One consistent theme is God's promise to be with his people, going back to Abraham (Gen. 17:8) and continuing with Moses (Ex. 3:12), Joshua (Josh. 1:5, 9), David (2 Samuel 7), Ezra (Ezra 7:6), Nehemiah (Neh. 2:8), and many others. The important promises to Abraham—sometimes called the "Abrahamic covenant"—included the land of Canaan (Gen. 12:7; 13:15; 17:8), many descendants (Gen. 12:2; 15:5), and blessings on Abraham and, through him, on the nations (Gen. 12:1–3). The Abrahamic covenant, then, forms the foundation of much that is in the Historical Books: (1) The stage on which the books unfold is the Promised Land of Canaan; (2) Israel became a mighty nation among its immediate neighbors, with thousands upon thousands of descendants of Abraham; and (3) Israel and Judah were repeatedly blessed when they followed God. Even non-Israelites were blessed when they turned to the

God of Abraham (e.g., Rahab in Joshua 2 and Naaman in 2 Kings 5). God did not forsake his promises to his people.

4. God's Kingdom: Both Divine and Human

The Bible teaches that God is king over the earth (e.g., Ex. 15:18; Ps. 93:1). As noted above, the exercise of his rule can be seen in his sovereignty over all nature, people, and nations.

God also chose to exercise his rule through human kings. As far back as Abraham's day, God had promised that kings would come from Abraham's line (Gen. 17:6, 16; 35:11; 49:10). He carefully prescribed that these kings should not be like the kings of neighboring nations, where warfare and foreign alliances were their primary features; by contrast, Israel's kings were to be rooted in a study of God's Word, and to let God fight Israel's battles (Deut. 17:14–20; Judg. 8:22–23; 1 Sam. 8:5, 20). The king was God's representative on earth, and God's earthly kingdom was entrusted to him. We can see this clearly in texts such as 2 Chronicles 13:8, which refers to "the kingdom of the LORD in the hand of the sons of David," and 1 Chronicles 29:23, where Solomon is chosen to sit "on the throne of the LORD."

God was a father to the Davidic kings, and they were "sons" of God in perpetuity (2 Sam. 7:11–16); these promises are known as the "Davidic covenant." While most of Israel's and Judah's kings did not live up to the ideals set out in Deuteronomy 17 and 2 Samuel 7, nevertheless the model was one where the king exercised his rule in connection with God's will and in dependence upon God. The New Testament highlights the kingdom theme as the ultimate "Son" of God was born from the lineage of David: Jesus, the Christ (Matt. 1:1; Rom. 1:3). It is with the proclamation of the kingdom that the Messiah's ministry commences (Matt. 4:17; Mark 1:14–15; Luke 4:16–21). With his resurrection and ascension Jesus began his reign as the Davidic king (Acts 13:33; Rom. 1:4), to carry out the long-awaited work of bringing light to the Gentiles (Matt. 28:1–20; Rom. 1:5). The church, now as Christ's representative presence in the world, is called in the power of the Spirit to proclaim and live out that kingdom reign (Acts 8:12; 19:8; 20:25).

5. God's Covenant: Reward and Punishment

The Abrahamic covenant required obedience to God in all realms of life. God said that Abraham had "obeyed my voice and kept my charge, my commandments, my statutes, and my laws" (Gen. 26:5). In other words, Abraham—who lived centuries before the Mosaic law was given at Mount Sinai—had lived his life in relationship with God in full accord with what later would be understood as keeping the law. The collections of Mosaic laws, and the attendant promises and obligations, have come to be known as the "Mosaic covenant," which spelled out how Israel was to shape the life of the nation under the Abrahamic covenant, which continued to be in effect through the promises of land, seed, and blessing to the nations (Gen. 12:1–3).

The book of Deuteronomy lays out most fully the rewards and punishments that would follow obedience or disobedience (Deuteronomy 27–28), and this perspective governed most of the writing of the Historical Books: when people followed the Lord, they were blessed, and when they did not, they suffered. We see this over and over again in Judges, 1–2 Samuel, 1–2 Kings, and 1–2 Chronicles. When the people turned from God, they suffered (e.g., Judges 2). The kings who sought the Lord, such as Hezekiah (2 Kings 18:7–8), were blessed, and punishment followed those who did not, such as Manasseh (2 Kings 24:3–4). In 1–2 Chronicles, especially, the author explicitly makes the connections between sin and punishment: see the accounts of Saul's death (1 Chron. 10:13) and Uzziah's leprosy (2 Chron. 26:16–23). As in Deuteronomy, the focus of these books is not so much on the individual person as on the moral condition of the people as a whole, with the king as their representative.

Distinctives

The largest single literary genre (type) in the Historical Books is prose narrative. Other genres are inserted in the narratives, including poetry (e.g., Judges 5; 1 Sam. 2:1–10; 2 Samuel 22; 1 Chron. 16:8–36), genealogies (e.g., Ruth 4:18–22; 1 Chronicles 1–9), lists (e.g., Joshua 13–21; 2 Sam. 23:8–39; 1 Kings 4:1–19; Ezra 2:1–70; 10:18–44; Nehemiah 11), letters (e.g., Ezra 4:11–22; 5:7–17; 6:2–22), and more. Prose narrative is found elsewhere in the Bible as well, not just in the Historical Books (e.g., all or parts of Genesis, Exodus, Numbers, Isaiah, Jeremiah, Ezekiel, Jonah, and Haggai, as well as the Gospels and Acts).

The historical narratives are presented as straightforward accounts of real events, and they treat miracles in the same narrative fashion as they do everyday events (e.g., the matter-of-fact mixing of the two in the Elijah and Elisha accounts). But narrative texts differ in several respects from poetic or prophetic texts. For example, as a rule, Hebrew narratives are not as selective as poetic texts (cf. the prose account of the Israelites' victory under Deborah in Judges 4 with the more sparse poetic account in Judges 5). Also, poetic texts can be much more figurative than prose texts (cf. Judg. 4:23–24 and 5:4–5, 20 on the Lord's victory; or Judg. 4:21 and 5:26–27 on the death of Sisera). In narrative, often the main story line is contained in the words of the characters, not in the prose narrative "framework" (e.g., Joshua 1 or 1 Samuel 8). Narrative texts are also usually concerned with past events, whereas prophetic texts are much more commonly present- or future-oriented.

Historical narratives are not, however, simply clusters of facts. Their authors used their God-given talents and creativity to tell the stories of real events from certain perspectives and to highlight certain facts and truths. The best way to see this is by comparing parallel accounts in 1–2 Kings and 1–2 Chronicles (in the same way in which one would compare parallel events in the Gospels); the authors of those books often relayed the same event from different, complementary perspectives, the later narrative sometimes borrowing directly from the earlier.

Notes on Critical Scholarship

Critical scholars (i.e., those whose chief concern is the origin and editorial history of the texts) in the past two centuries have provided many helpful insights into the nature, composition, and messages of the Historical Books. This should not surprise us, since all truth is God's truth. However, many critical scholars have also been profoundly skeptical of the Bible's claims, and so their results must be weighed carefully.

For example, one common theory postulates that the books of Deuteronomy through 2 Kings (minus Ruth) were editorially shaped during the exile to explain why Israel and Judah had fallen. This theory helpfully highlights many themes from Deuteronomy that are played out in the Historical Books. However, it can be used to loosen the connection of Deuteronomy with Moses (which the Bible affirms), and it is skeptical about the authorial integrity of most books as they stand today.

Many scholars today also seriously question the historical reliability of almost everything in the Historical Books. The most extreme scholars deny that any of the events described in the Historical Books took place, and they claim that all of the books were written after the exile. Other scholars are less skeptical than that but still deny that many events occurred (e.g., all the miracles, and the events before the time of Solomon). Evangelical scholars have provided helpful responses to such skeptics.

4

Introduction to the Poetic and Wisdom Literature

David Reimer

Poetry is pervasive in the Hebrew Bible—the only books in the Old Testament without any poetry are Leviticus, Ruth, Esther, Haggai, and Malachi (although 1 Kings and Nehemiah could perhaps be added to this list). In order to be a competent reader of Scripture, one must have some understanding of the nature and conventions of Old Testament poetry: What is it? How does it work? Who wrote it?

Even in English it is not always a simple matter to distinguish poetry from prose. Often the reader is simply guided by the lay-out of the text: in poetry, each line of poetry has its own line of text; in prose, there are no special line breaks. No such convention can be seen in our oldest biblical Hebrew manuscripts, and only with the work of the medieval Jewish scribes were biblical texts presented in a manner that distinguishes prose and poetry.

"Poets" in Ancient Israel?

If the boundary between prose and poetry is sometimes difficult to discern, so too are the traces of poets in the archaeological record of ancient Israel. While the nations of Israel and Judah had functioning bureaucracies and civil servants as well as a temple complex that required administration and accounts, little explicit evidence remains for the education of the people who filled these positions or for the milieu in which they would have matured and flourished. There is enough to know there was a literate scribal class, but not enough to say how they became such.

In biblical literature, the concerns of poetry and scribes come together. In addition to the Psalms, the biblical Wisdom Books are also books of poetry, and the poets and sages who were responsible for them belonged to that scribal class (e.g., see Prov. 25:1). Even if the extrabiblical record of their activity is minimal, their contribution to the writings that became the Scripture of Israel is immense. Wherever poetry is found in the Bible, one finds literary reflection in the service of worship and godly living.

What Is Hebrew "Poetry"?

Poetry is commonly recognized by lines exhibiting rhythm and rhyme, readily exemplified by nursery rhymes: even the simple "one, two, buckle my shoe" demonstrates both aspects. This brief snippet exhibits rhythm (*óne, twó,* [pause] *búckle my shóe*), terseness, assonance (the resemblance of the vowel sounds in "one" and "buckle", and "two" and "shoe"), and rhyme—and this sort of wordcraft can also be seen in the work of the ancient Hebrew poets. Apart from rhyme, conventions such as terse expression, freedom in word order, and an absence of typical prose particles also distinguish biblical Hebrew poetry from prose.

One prominent feature of biblical poetry not found in English poems is that of the "seconding sequence"; that is, a line of Hebrew poetry generally has two parts. The poet's art allows the relationship between those parts to be crafted in manifold ways. Here is Psalm 19:1:

> The heavens declare the glory of God,
>> and the sky above proclaims his handiwork.

> *Hashamayim mesapperim kebod 'El*
>> *Uma'aseh yadaw maggid haraqia'*

In the opening of Psalm 19, *the heavens* in the first part finds an echo in *the sky above* in the second part; likewise, *declare* parallels *proclaims*, and *the glory of God* partners *his handiwork*. With nearly one-to-one correspondence, it is obvious why such poetic parallelism has often been called "synonymous"—one of three such categories, the others being "antithetical," where the second part provides the opposite to the first part (e.g., "A wise son makes a glad father, but a foolish son is a sorrow to his mother," Prov. 10:1), and "synthetic," where the two parts of the line do not display either of these kinds of semantic relationship.

Assigning a line of poetry to one of these simple categories represents only a first small step in discerning the poet's art. This "parallel" structure offers the poet a surprisingly rich framework for artistic development: the poet is not simply saying the same thing twice in slightly different terms. The parallel line structure provided Hebrew poets with a means of exploiting similarity and difference on the levels of *sound*, *syntax*, and *semantics* to achieve an artistically compelling expression of their vision. Unfortunately, of these three elements, the first two (sound and syntax) usually do not survive translation. In the Hebrew of Psalm 19:1, both parts of the line are roughly eleven/twelve syllables, with three stresses in the first part, and four in the second. Syntactically, they form a very neat "envelope" structure, of the a-b-c/c'-b'-a' pattern: subject-verb-object/object-verb-subject. Such symmetry already begins to express the totality of the poet's vision.

However, semantics—the meanings of words—are observable in translation. Of course, complete overlap of the meanings of words cannot be sustained across languages, so there is still an advantage to those who can enjoy the poetry in its original setting. While the simple matches across the parts of this first line of Psalm 19 were noted above, there is yet more to be observed. The a:a' pair ("heavens" and "sky above") are not precise synonyms. "Heavens" is the more generic term, and occurs well over four hundred times in the Old Testament; by contrast, "sky above" (Hb. *raqia'*) occurs only seventeen times, and nine of those are in the creation account of Genesis 1. Even in this apparently simple development, which exploits the seconding pattern of the parallel line structure, the poet moves from the more generic assertion in the first part to the more specific in the second to display God's glory in his creative acts ("handiwork"). (Confirmation of this allusion to creation comes in Ps. 19:4, which partners "earth" and "world" so that Ps. 19:1 and Ps. 19:4 together allude to the "heavens and earth" of Gen. 1:1.) Something similar could be noted of the verbs: "declare" (Hb. *mesapperim*) refers to the simple act of rehearsal or recounting; "proclaim" (Hb. *maggid*) on the other hand brings the nuance of announcement, of revelation, of news. This invitation to savor the wonder of creation's wordless confession of the glories of God (Ps. 19:1–4a), then, forms a profound counterpart to the famous reflection on the verbal expressions of the will of the Lord found in the law (Ps. 19:7–11).

Many lines of Hebrew verse do not offer *this* kind of parallel correspondence, however. Sometimes simple grammatical dependency binds the parts together (e.g., Ps. 19:3), or the first part asks a question that the second part answers (Ps. 19:12). Sometimes there is a narrative development (Ps. 19:5, 13), sometimes an escalation or intensification of terms (Ps. 19:1, 10). These few examples are drawn from a single psalm with fairly regular features; surveying the entire poetic corpus would add a myriad of possibilities. Consistently, however, the art and craft of the Bible's poems offers an invitation to read slowly, to have one's vision broadened, one's perception deepened—or, as it was put above, to see literary reflection in the service of worship and godly living.

Where Is Poetry Found in the Old Testament?

Poetry is pervasive throughout the Old Testament, in spite of the fact there is no word in biblical Hebrew for "poem." The medieval Jewish scholars responsible for the accentuation of the Hebrew text of the Bible used a distinct notation for Psalms, Job, and Proverbs (their order in the Hebrew Bible) that marked these books as "poetic." However, as figure 4.1 shows, Hebrew terms may refer to a particular kind of poem, and thus illustrate their wide diffusion. As this simple (and partial) list demonstrates, poetry is at home in every part of Israelite life.

Songs and prayers of praise and lament most naturally cluster in the book of Psalms, although they can be found elsewhere in the Old Testament as well (e.g., 2 Samuel 22 [and Psalm 18]; 1 Chronicles 16; Habakkuk 3). There is considerable overlap here, with some of the "epic poetry" found in the Pentateuch (e.g., Genesis 49; Exodus 15; Deuteronomy 32; 33) and beyond (Judges 5). Wisdom and "song" often come together (e.g., Ps. 49:4), and the parallel structure of the Hebrew poetic line was a perfect vehicle for proverbial sayings (Proverbs 10–31). Likewise, the dialogues of the book of Job (Job 3–41) are formed entirely in poetry. The book of Lamentations contains a collection of *qinah* poems, whose acrostic structure also forges a connection to a "wisdom" form of composition. The term *massa'* points to a connection with the Hebrew prophets, whose oracles were normally delivered in verse form. The greater part of Isaiah–Malachi is written in poetry: while definitions of a "prophet" may vary, the writing prophets at any rate may at least be said to be poets.

**Fig. 4.1 Hebrew Terms for
Types of Poems**

Category	Hebrew Term	Meaning
General	*shir*	song
	tehillah	prayer, song of praise
	zamir/zimrah	song
	qinah	lament, dirge, with a grieving content
wisdom sayings	*mashal*	proverb
	khidah	riddle
prophetic poetry	*massa'*	oracular utterance, "burden"

What Is Hebrew "Wisdom"?

Hebrew "wisdom" is readily recognized but difficult to define. Some choose simply to define "wisdom" by the literature that best represents it, so that it becomes a list of books. Since wisdom concerns are scattered widely throughout the Bible, this approach is unhelpfully restrictive. Others choose to define "wisdom" as an outlook, almost a philosophy of life. But different "wisdom" writers have differing emphases, so this approach seems too fragmentary. Further, the wisdom writings are of varied character themselves: there is the instructional or proverbial wisdom of Proverbs (basic instructions in how to live), the contemplative wisdom of Job and Ecclesiastes (pondering the perplexing side of life), and the lyric wisdom of the Song of Solomon (a story celebrating one of God's best gifts). What the books and outlooks have in common, however, is a keen interest in the way the world works, humanity's place within it, and how all this operates under God's creative, sovereign care. Biblical "wisdom," then, might be defined as *skill in the art of godly living, or more fully, that orientation which allows one to live in harmonious accord with God's ordering of the world.* And "Wisdom Literature" consists of those writings that reflect on or inform that orientation.

Unlike psalmody, wisdom does not have an exclusive relationship with poetry. There are wisdom strands throughout the Old

Testament. The "court" stories of Joseph, Esther, and Daniel, for example, all might be said to be "embodied" wisdom. The special connection with the court of Solomon (see esp. 1 Kings 3:1–28; 4:29–34) is well known, and Solomon may be seen as the "patron" of wisdom in the Old Testament (see Prov. 1:1; 10:1; 25:1; Song 1:1; and by implication Eccles. 1:1). Unlike Job and Proverbs, Ecclesiastes' unique content is communicated in a distinctive style that often defies a simple prose/poetry categorization. By contrast, the lyrical lines of the Song of Solomon's expressions of love are clearly poetic, but its content stands slightly apart from that typical of the "wisdom" books. Some psalms are devoted to "wisdom" themes (e.g., Psalms 37; 49; 73) and show how keeping the law in joyful response to God's goodness (e.g., Psalms 1; 19; 119) is the epitome of wise living.

Contexts for Wisdom and Poetry

Given the preceding discussion, the social setting of wisdom writing would by definition be among those of the literate class, and this in turn suggests a setting within the social elite. It is no surprise, then, that wisdom literature finds a strong connection to the royal court, or that the hymnic poetry of the Psalms (associated with David, Jerusalem, and the temple) likewise has pronounced royal overtones. On the other hand, many of the proverbs do not require high-status origins; rather, they more naturally can be thought of as "folk wisdom," which places their social milieu within the home or clan. It is helpful to distinguish here between wisdom *writing*, which requires scribal education, and wisdom more generally, which could be found at any level of society.

Poetic conventions and wisdom reflections were not unique to Israel in the ancient Near East. The discovery of the Ugaritic texts, found at modern Ras Shamra on the coast of Syria in 1929 and fully deciphered by the end of 1930, revealed a poetic literature dating to the second half of the second millennium BC whose diction shared much with the poetry of the Hebrew Bible. Their discovery stimulated renewed study of biblical Hebrew poetry. The literary remains of Israel's neighbors have also provided striking parallels to the wisdom literature. Egyptian "instruction" literature evokes strong resonances with Proverbs, the best-known being that of *The Instruction of Amenemope* (c. thirteenth century BC), which has marked similarities to Proverbs 22:17–24:22. Cuneiform texts from Mesopotamia stretching back into the third millennium BC wrestle with the problem of the "righteous sufferer" in a manner comparable to the book of Job. There are also points of contact with Aramaic wisdom literature, and parallels may even be drawn with later Greek writings. Some students of the Scriptures are bothered by the parallels with extrabiblical literature. What sense does it make to speak in terms of "inspiration," when much of Psalm 104, for example, seems to be shared with Egyptian hymnody? Or when the struggles of Job are paralleled in part by Mesopotamian "righteous sufferer" stories? Here it must be remembered that inspiration is not simply a matter of forms, motifs, or structures, but of *content* that uses various existing forms in a way that accurately reveals the true and living God and his will for his people.

Two advantages in particular are gained by noting such extrabiblical parallels. (1) They demonstrate that the Bible's inspired authors both *inhabit* and *challenge* their contemporary cultural milieu. The questions of ancient Israelites about life were not so very different from the questions of ancient Egyptians, or Sumerians, or Syrians. To that extent, these cross-connections illustrate the degree to which ancient Israel participated in the wider culture of the ancient Near East. Israel and Judah are sometimes portrayed as if they were a "backwater," tucked away in a corner of their world, but such literary parallels show their high level of cultural integration. (2) On the other hand, the writers of biblical wisdom were no mere imitators, producing derivative echoes of their cosmopolitan neighbors. In terms of *scope*, *originality*, and *profundity*, the biblical writings remain unrivaled. Indeed, one of the small mysteries about them—Job, Psalms, and Proverbs in particular—is just why they are written on such a grand scale. In terms of range and depth of vision, they far transcend their non-biblical parallels, their outlook reflecting the greatness of the God who informs and indeed shapes them. Awareness of the distinctive contours of biblical poetry and wisdom sharpens our understanding of the insights and concerns of Israel's poets and sages.

Poetic and wisdom literature tends to resist a straightforward chronological setting. Rightly understanding the Bible's histories and prophetic literature depends to an extent on taking their historical context into account; such is not normally the case for Israel's hymns and wisdom. Evidence from the ancient Near East demonstrates that hymnic and wisdom writings are among the most ancient of literary deposits, and likewise some of the Bible's poetic compositions may be among its oldest. But it is also clear that throughout the histories of Israel and Judah, Hebrew poets and sages were at work—from earliest days, on past the canonical compositions, up through the Hellenistic period in the post-canonical books of *Sirach* and *Wisdom of Solomon* and beyond. Their writings often defy a precise historical setting. To take one example at random, a saying like "Whoever plans to do evil will be called a schemer" (Prov. 24:8) requires no precise historical context, nor do we have the evidence to give it one. While particular poems and prayers (e.g., Psalm 137) may be tied to a given historical circumstance, such cases remain the exception.

Unifying Themes

Each of the books included in this overarching introduction has distinctive content. Still, in these poetic strands of the Bible, whether inclined toward wisdom or hymnody, there are a number of themes that surface repeatedly. Only a few of the most prominent are discussed here.

The *fear of the Lord* provides a pervasive orientation throughout the Psalms and Wisdom Books. The phrase, or one like it, appears about sixty times in these books, but its significance goes beyond its simple frequency. It also sets the framework in which wise living takes place. So in the book of Job it becomes the leading question of the outer frame of the book (Job 1:9). It nearly brackets the entire collection of the Psalms: the first injunction in the Psalms directs rulers to "serve the LORD with fear" (Ps. 2:11), while to fear the Lord gives one pleasure (Ps. 145:19). Proverbs is permeated with this outlook: not only is "the fear of the LORD . . . the beginning of knowledge" (Prov. 1:7), but so too it is "a fountain of life" (Prov. 14:27). Even the apparently skeptical Ecclesiastes joins in, since whatever else may happen, "God is the one you must fear" (Eccles. 5:7; see 8:12; 12:13).

The *limits of human wisdom* form the natural counterpart to the fear of God. To be sure, there is something about "wisdom" that implies a depth of understanding, in particular of how God has ordered the world and how to live in accord with that divine ordering. The characterization of Solomon's wisdom as being that of a proto-natural scientist (1 Kings 4:33) points in this direction and sheds light on the nature lesson the Lord gave Job (esp. in Job 38–39). This already implies limits to human wisdom, however, and the two strands (fear of God; human limitations) come together powerfully in Job 28. Again this outlook also informs Ecclesiastes. The several "who knows?" texts point in this direction (e.g., Eccles. 3:21; 6:12), as does the reflection on oath taking (Eccles. 5:2). Contrary to modern secular humanist claims, this is no denigration of human dignity: it is rather to recognize the context in which human freedom is most fully realized (cf. Psalm 8; also Pss. 16:1–11; 108:1–6; etc.).

This literature reflects on *the righteous and the wicked in relation to God*. This is an ancient problem (see Gen. 18:23), and lies at the heart of the first psalm's evocative portrait of the nature and prospects of the "righteous" contrasting with the fate of the "wicked" (Ps. 1:5–6), a contrast worked out in a sustained way in Psalms 37 and 73. The bulk of the dialogues of Job turn on rightly assessing Job's character and how this places him in relationship to God. Many proverbs observe the behavior of the righteous and wicked, and the outcomes their actions bring; such reflections are especially dense in Proverbs 10–12, as the collection of axioms gets under way following the book's extended introduction. As the psalmist of Psalm 73 and the "Preacher" (*Qoheleth* in Ecclesiastes) noted, the simple correlation of God's rewarding the righteous and punishing the wicked does not always seem to hold (see Eccles. 7:15), and so a question of justice is raised, and with it the problem of evil—one of the deepest mysteries faced by people of faith.

This leads in turn to the way in which these books *grapple with suffering*. Naturally, interest here gravitates to the book of Job. Interpreters differ over just what solution the book offers, but there can be little doubt that a resolution is achieved in the presence of the Creator, the only place where the meaning of human suffering can be understood. But beyond this, many psalms voice a lament ("lament" providing the largest single category of psalm "type") that gives voice to this crisis before God (e.g., Psalms 3; 4; 6; 10; 13). Even the only subliminally theological Song of Solomon expresses not only the delights of love satisfied but the agonies of love unfulfilled (e.g., Song 5:6–8; cf. 8:6–7).

Given that the thread of life before God is woven through each of these books, a further common theme is *the nature of true piety.* The interest of the book of Job in this question was already seen above: is it possible to worship God with integrity (cf. Satan's question in Job 1:9)? One of the designs of the narrative is to answer this question in the affirmative. Again, virtually the whole of the Psalter quite naturally sings of worship with integrity (e.g., Psalms 25; 26; 31; 84).

5

Introduction to the Prophetic Books

Paul House

Mesopotamian texts indicate that long before Israel entered Canaan, other countries had prophets. These texts from Israel's neighbors indicate that their prophets claimed to intercede for people to the gods, speak for the gods, criticize the people's moral and ethical deficiencies on behalf of the gods, predict future events through special knowledge given by the gods, and denounce enemies by the power of the gods. Though the Bible asserts belief in one God, not many gods, it basically portrays Israel's prophets fulfilling the same tasks. This is not surprising if the idea of a "prophet" was of a person who spoke for a god to the people.

The Old Testament includes three basic terms for the concept of "prophet," two of which have a similar connotation. First, on a few occasions the Old Testament uses the terms *hozeh* or *ro'eh*. The former means "visionary," while the latter means "seer." These words imply that prophets were people who could "envision" or "see" things others could not. They could "see" or "envision" details about the present as well as what God wanted in the future. For example, Saul expected the "seer" Samuel to know where some lost donkeys had gone (1 Sam. 9:1–10). Samuel could indeed "see" where the donkeys had gone, but he could also "see" that God had chosen Saul to rule Israel (1 Sam. 9:15–17). Saul expected to pay the "seer" something for his trouble. Such expectations and the greed of some individuals calling themselves prophets eventually led people to think that all seers were after money (see Amos 7:12).

Second, the Old Testament most commonly uses the word *nabi'* for "prophet." The origins of this word are uncertain; perhaps it comes from a root that means "to announce," which could imply that a prophet was one who announced or declared vital information. In any event the prophet serves as a spokesman: in Exodus 7:1 Moses will be like God to Pharaoh, while Aaron will be his prophet (i.e., his spokesman). Indeed, Israelite prophets claimed to declare the words of Yahweh, the God of Israel, while in other lands the prophets claimed to speak the words of other gods. Since so many prophets were active and were declaring conflicting messages, people had to determine who actually spoke for God and who was a false prophet.

The prophets addressed both future and present issues, with present issues often being the overwhelming concern of their messages. They did announce future events, such as the Messiah's coming and the final day of judgment, but typically they declared how God's people should live in light of their covenant with God (see below).

The Prophets in Israel's History

The Bible indicates that prophets who served the one true living God existed well before the careers of the writing prophets. Abraham (as early as 2000 BC), Moses (as early as 1450), Samuel (c. 1050–1010), Nathan (c. 1010–970), Elijah and Elisha (c. 860–850), and Huldah (627) are but a few of the persons whom Genesis–Psalms calls prophets.

Through Moses, God revealed his standards for prophets. According to Deuteronomy 13:1–11, Israel's prophets must never teach the people to serve any other god but Yahweh. Even if a prophet can perform signs and wonders, the people must not follow him if he advocates serving other gods. In Deuteronomy 18:9–22 Moses adds that other nations will have prophets who tell the future and communicate with spirits (Deut. 18:9–14); in contrast, God will put his own words in his prophets' mouths (Deut. 18:18). Further, a prophet can show that he has God's authorization by speaking the truth about future events (Deut. 18:21–22). Israel must wait for the perfect prophet whom God will send (see Acts 3:22–23). As they wait, they must obey prophets who proclaim faithfulness to God's covenant with Israel and whose predictions come true every time. Any prophet failing to meet these standards does not speak for God.

It is important to recognize that the prophets were not the regular teachers of God's word—that was the priests' calling (Deut. 33:10). Rather, God raised up prophets for particular times in the Old Testament story (which is why their "calls" were so important, as in Isaiah 6).

The first Prophetic Books originated in the eighth century BC. These books came about during the decline of the kingdoms of Israel and Judah and the rise of Assyria as a world power. Eventually Assyria destroyed Israel in 722 BC, leaving only Judah as a remnant of David's kingdom. Hosea, Amos, and Jonah all ministered at mid-century (760–745 BC). Hosea and Amos decried social injustice fueled by covenantal disobedience and warned the covenant people and the nations of a future "day of the Lord," a day of judgment for their sins. Jonah reluctantly preached to Nineveh, the capital of Assyria, before Assyria became a dominant, oppressing nation. Isaiah, the greatest prophet of this era, shared his predecessors' concerns for sin and judgment and wrote some of the Bible's richest promises of a future Savior and his kingdom. Isaiah's book contains decades of writing (c. 745–690 BC). Micah ministered near the end of the century (overlapping with Isaiah), rebuking Judah for personal and societal sins and (like Isaiah) predicting God's victory over Assyria during the Sennacherib crisis of 701 BC (see 2 Kings 18–19). Micah promised that a leader born in Bethlehem would defeat God's enemies (Mic. 5:1–5; see Matt. 2:1–12).

Seventh-century BC prophets wrote against the background of the continuing power and ultimate demise of Assyria, which by 612 BC had lost its place as the world's greatest power to Babylon. These prophets pressed God's claims on the chosen people, especially the standards of the Mosaic covenant. Zephaniah (c. 640–609 BC) denounced Judah's worship of other gods, warned of judgment, and promised renewal beyond judgment. Nahum (c. 660–630 BC) announced the end of Assyria's tyranny, and Habakkuk (c. 640–609) explored the ways of God in the days leading up to Babylon's capturing of Judah. Of course, Jeremiah also worked during this century and well into the next. He declared God's word of repentance to Judah for at least forty years (627–587 BC; Jer. 1:1–3), decades that spanned from the period when Judah still had time to change its ways and avoid punishment, to the destruction of Jerusalem by Babylon in 587 and the subsequent exiling of the people. He repeatedly preached repentance, yet his most famous words are the promise of a future new covenant with the house of Israel (Jer. 31:31–34; see Heb. 8:8–12).

Sixth-century BC prophets lived under the shadow of exile. A few of them also lived during the shifting of world domination from Babylon to Persia, which occurred in 538 BC. Daniel was taken to Babylon in 605 BC. He worked there until at least 536 BC. Ezekiel joined the exiles in Babylon in 597 BC, where he wrote accounts of visions he received during 593–571. Both of these exiles envisioned perilous times and future days of glory for God's people. Obadiah witnessed the terrors of Babylon's invasion of Judah in 587 BC. Haggai and Zechariah were among the people allowed to return to Jerusalem from Persia in 520–516 BC. They participated in the rebuilding of the temple and looked forward to future glory for God's people under the Messiah's leadership.

Malachi served during the fifth century BC. A contemporary of Ezra and Nehemiah (c. 460–425 BC), he experienced the problems associated with rebuilding Jerusalem and restoring faithful worship and covenantal obedience. Malachi identified flaws in the returned exiles' commitment to God, such as insincere worship, the failure of the priests to teach God's Word, and marital infidelity (Mal. 1:6–2:16). He also predicted the coming of a new Elijah and the Messiah (Mal. 4:5–6). The book of Joel probably comes from this period as well, as it makes no mention of a king in Judah. Joel calls the people to repentance at a time of national calamity (a locust plague).

Prophetic Books

Little is known about the Prophetic Books' composition and preservation, though some helpful information may be gleaned from the biblical text. For example, Isaiah had disciples who were able to preserve his words (Isa. 8:16), and Jeremiah's disciple Baruch was a scribe who wrote down some of the prophet's messages (Jer. 36:1–32). Many prophets were probably able to write their own words (Isa. 8:1–2; Jer. 1:4–19), since literacy was fairly widespread.

The prophets' words were originally copied on papyrus or leather scrolls that were passed on to future generations by persons who valued them (Jer. 36:1–4). Several such books existed at one time, for the author of 1–2 Chronicles reports sources composed by or about prophets (1 Chron. 29:29; 2 Chron. 9:29; 26:22). By Jeremiah's time the prophecy of Micah had been handed down and was considered authoritative (Jer. 26:18, quoting Mic. 3:12). According to the apocryphal book *Sirach*, by the second century BC (at the very latest) all the Prophetic Books were considered authoritative Scripture (see *Sir.* 48:22; 49:6, 8, 12; cf. *1 Macc.* 2:60).

Many types of literature appear in the Prophetic Books. There are narratives detailing what the prophets did and the circumstances in which they received and delivered their messages. There are also sermons, extended poems, dialogues between God and prophets, and visionary experiences. All of these forms reveal the great themes noted in the next section, and these themes provide the books' plots (or story lines) and major characters.

Unifying Themes in the Prophetic Books

The Prophetic Books include most of the Old Testament's greatest themes, preserving in written form for future generations the reasons Israel's history happened as it did. Though the authors wrote in different times and under different circumstances, their messages are in theological harmony with one another and with other types of biblical books. Several interrelated ideas unify the prophetic message, making it possible for readers to find their bearings in some difficult literature. It is often helpful to decide which of the following themes the biblical author is stressing when one becomes puzzled by the content of the books.

First, *the prophets assert that God has spoken through them.* They clearly considered themselves God's messengers and heralds, for they repeatedly preface their messages with the phrase, "Thus says Yahweh." In this way the prophets are claiming that their books are the written word of God. Peter explains that the prophets "were carried along by the Holy Spirit" (2 Pet. 1:21).

Just as God used Moses to write and preach so that Israel could know God's will in his era, so God used the prophets in their generations. The prophets declared God's instructions in two basic ways: word and symbol. Usually the prophets presented God's word orally (e.g., Jer. 7:1–8:3) or in written form (e.g., Jer. 36:1–32) to varying types and sizes of audiences. Occasionally they performed symbolic acts that demonstrated God's purposes. For example, Isaiah went naked and barefoot for three years to teach God's people their future if they continued to seek help from other nations rather than from God (Isa. 20:1–6). Perhaps the saddest case of symbolic prophecy was Hosea's marriage to unfaithful Gomer, which portrayed God's relationship with unfaithful Israel (Hosea 1–3).

Second, *the prophets affirm that God chose Israel for covenant relationship.* The Pentateuch (the first five books of the Old Testament) teaches that God chose Abraham and his family to bless all nations (Gen. 12:1–9), that he revealed salvation by grace to Abraham (Gen. 15:6), and that he assigned Moses to write a record of this revelation (Ex. 24:4). Furthermore, through Moses in Exodus–Deuteronomy he revealed the lifestyle that reflects that relationship. With these truths in mind, the prophets addressed Israel as a people with special responsibilities based on this special relationship (Jeremiah 2–6; Hosea 1–3; Amos 2:6–3:8; etc.). Through the prophets God revealed the success and failure of Israel's attempts or lack of attempts to fulfill their confession of faith in God and their God-given role as a kingdom of priests charged with serving the nations (see Ex. 19:5–6).

Third, sadly, *the prophets most often report that the majority of Israel has sinned against their God and his standards for their relationship.* They have failed to trust God (Isa. 7:1–14). Thus, they have broken the Ten Commandments (see Ex. 20:1–17 and Jer. 7:1–15; Hos. 4:2). They have worshiped other gods (Ezek. 8:1–18). They have mistreated one another and failed to preserve justice among God's people (Isa. 1:21–31). They have refused to repent (Amos 4:6–11). Of course, in these times there was always a faithful minority, called the "remnant" (see Isa. 4:3; 10:20–22; etc.), as the prophets' ministries themselves demonstrate (see Hebrews 11).

Fourth, *the prophets warn that judgment will eradicate sin.* This judgment is often called the "day of the Lord" (Isa. 2:12–22; Joel 2:1–11; Zeph. 1:7–18; Amos 5:18–20; etc.). This is a day in history, as when Jerusalem was destroyed by Babylon (Jer. 42:18), but it is also a day to come, when God will judge all the world's inhabitants (Isa. 24:1–23). The prophets recorded these warnings in writing so readers can do what the prophets' original audience usually failed to do—turn from sin to God.

Fifth, *the prophets promise that renewal lies beyond the day of punishment that has occurred already in history and beyond the coming day that will bring history as we know it to a close.* The coming of the Savior lies beyond the destruction of Israel and other such events. He will rule Israel and the nations, and he will bring peace and righteousness to the world (Isa. 9:2–7; 11:1–16). This Savior must suffer, die, and rise from the dead (Isa. 52:13–53:12). He will be "like a son of man," and "the Ancient of Days" (God himself) will give him all the kingdoms of the world (Dan. 7:9–14). He will be the catalyst for a new covenant with Israel that will include all those, Jew or Gentile, whom God's Spirit fills and changes (Jer. 31:31–40; Ezek. 34:25–31; 36:22–32). This new people will serve him faithfully. Eventually he will cleanse the world of sin and recreate the earth (Isa. 65:17–25; 66:18–24; Zeph. 3:8–20). The creation now spoiled by sin will be whole again.

Scholarly Issues and the Prophetic Books

The past two centuries have seen many debates concerning the Prophetic Books. These discussions include many facets but may be summarized in the following categories: unity, authenticity, and relationship to the New Testament.

For centuries most scholars basically accepted that the Prophetic Books were written by the persons whose names were mentioned at the beginning of the books (Isa. 1:1; Jer. 1:1–3; etc.). They did so because they held traditional beliefs about the inspiration and authority of the Bible (see Ps. 19:1–14; 2 Tim. 3:14–17; 2 Pet. 1:21) yet also because the books are as well attested by other ancient sources, and as coherent in content and style, as any surviving ancient books.

Beginning in the late 1700s, however, several scholars began to argue that differences within individual books indicate that they were not composed of the words of the persons that the books name as the source of the material. For example, they noted that the book of Isaiah stresses judgment and renewal, mentions Assyria and Babylon as conquerors of Israel, and describes exile and return from exile. Therefore, they posited at least two authors, one who lived in the eighth century BC and one who lived in the sixth century, with perhaps a third in the fifth century. They soon made similar arguments about other prophetic books. As they continued to find other differences, they suggested still more authors. By the early 1900s such scholars wrote freely about the "authentic" passages (written or spoken by the persons the Bible names as authors) and the "inauthentic" passages (written by later editors of the books).

Many of these critical scholars also concluded that the Old Testament prophets did not predict future events in the manner the New Testament claims. Rather, in their view the prophets wrote about events of their own day, but New Testament writers applied these texts to Jesus, the church, and other subjects. Thus, the unity of the Old Testament and the New Testament, which Jesus and Paul are portrayed as affirming (Matt. 5:17–20; John 5:45–46; 10:35; 2 Tim. 3:14–17), simply does not exist. Church tradition may treat the Bible as a unity, but, they argued, historical research does not confirm that belief.

Evangelical scholars responded to these trends in several ways. First, they reaffirmed their belief in the inspiration and authority of the Bible and in the Holy Spirit's ability to provide information on the future to the prophets. Second, they observed that the Old Testament and New Testament writers—the closest witnesses to the time of the books' writing and the most ancient teachers of that word—never name any writers of a biblical book other than the ones listed in the Old Testament. Third, they offered treatments of the books that explained how the passages in question could come from the time period the books mention. Fourth, they described how the New Testament writers used the Old Testament books in a contextual, not arbitrary, manner.

Recently evangelical scholars have been joined by less traditional experts in their critique of many of these assertions by critical scholars. These experts believe that differences in emphasis in a book do not necessarily mean different authors, since an author may stress many diverging themes that eventually constitute a unified composition. For instance, in order for a Greek comedy to end happily, there must be some negative reality overcome. For a Greek tragedy to end sadly, there must be some joy lost. Similarly, the prophetic message included punishment on the way to renewal and sin that marred the nation's once-positive relationship with God. The presence of different concepts helps comprise the whole; it does not necessitate multiple authors.

Despite this emerging agreement on the unified content of the Prophetic Books, evangelical scholars and their counterparts still often disagree on how the books came together. Many evangelical scholars continue to hold to the unity of the books as the words of the prophets that the books themselves identify, while their dialogue partners believe that the unity came about through the careful work of editors over a long period of time. What remains at stake in these discussions is the truthfulness of the text's claims to originate from a particular person in a particular era, addressing items specific to that era as well as items in the future. It is the special calling of the particular prophet that gives his writing canonical authority for God's people (Deut. 18:18–19).

Pronouns in the Prophets

As prepositions are to the letters of Paul, so pronouns are to the oracles of the prophets: crucial for meaning, but often puzzling. Hebrew prophets delivered messages on God's behalf, so identifying who is being addressed, and who is being spoken about, is central to understanding their preaching. Naturally, use of pronouns ("I," "we," "you," "she," etc.) can frustrate modern readers when their *antecedent* (the actual person or entity being referred to) either is missing or could have more than one possible candidate. Although pronoun confusion arises most naturally in the Prophets, it also crops up in the prayers of the Psalms. Sometimes modern biblical translations smooth out such difficulties for the reader by specifying the referent or adjusting the pronouns. The ESV approach, in general, prefers to represent the pronouns in English as equivalent to those appearing in the Hebrew, and not to make decisions for the reader about their referents.

In prophetic literature, confusing pronoun references occur especially in the following cases: (1) unmarked interjections; (2) unsignaled transitions in oracles or other passages; (3) differences in ancient and modern conventions for pronouns; and (4) obscurity in a passage beyond simply its pronouns. Also, (5) an author might be addressing the people as a whole (personified as a single "you"). The following are examples for each scenario.

(1) Who is "he" in Zechariah 10:11?

> He shall pass through the sea of troubles
>> and strike down the waves of the sea,
>> and all the depths of the Nile shall be dried up.
> The pride of Assyria shall be laid low,
>> and the scepter of Egypt shall depart.

The Lord speaks as "I" on either side of this verse; ancient versions and commentators often read "they" here, to link back to the last word of Zechariah 10:10. However, the context suggests that the action of Zechariah 10:10 belongs to the Lord, and in Zechariah 10:12b, the Lord's own voice seems to refer to himself in the third person ("his name"). Here the prophet's voice and the Lord's seem fused, and in spite of changing between "I" and "he/him," the reference is consistently to God.

(2) Who is "us" in Isaiah 41:22?

> Let them bring them, and tell us
>> what is to happen.
> Tell us the former things, what they are,
>> that we may consider them,
> that we may know their outcome;
>> or declare to us the things to come.

The first-person plural reference continues in Isaiah 41:23, and then reappears in Isaiah 41:26, but never with an explicit referent. Here, help comes from the wider context. The setting is the divine courtroom ("set forth your case," Isa. 41:21), and this is introduced at Isaiah 41:1 ("let us draw near for judgment"), so "us" in Isaiah 41:22 remains the members of the divine court who are hearing the case against the idols of Isaiah 41:7.

(3) Who is "her" in Micah 7:10?

> Then my enemy will see,
>> and shame will cover her who said to me,
>> "Where is the LORD your God?"
> My eyes will look upon her;
>> now she will be trampled down
>> like the mire of the streets.

The answer partly depends on who is "me" in Micah 7:8. "My enemy" in Micah 7:8, 10 is grammatically feminine (Heb. *'oyabti*), and so is the antecedent for "her" in Micah 7:10. It is likely, then, that the first-person voice is also feminine (see Mic. 6:9; 7:11)—Jerusalem personified. In biblical convention, cities are referred to as feminine and nations as masculine—unlike modern English usage in which cities are normally neuter ("it") and nations are feminine.

(4) A genuine difficulty is the "they" (fem.) reference of Ezekiel 30:17 ("The young men of On and of Pi-beseth shall fall by the sword, and the women shall go into captivity."), represented in the ESV by "women" but with a textual note, "Or *the cities*; Hebrew *they*." The translation adopted in the text takes its cue from "young men" in Ezekiel 30:17a and "daughters" of Ezekiel 30:18b. "Cities" remains possible (see example 3), as "On" and "Pi-beseth" are the closest immediate antecedents in context.

(5) The prophets can personify God's people, viewed corporately, as if a single person. In Isaiah 41:8–10, "you" (masculine singular) refers to "Jacob," the whole people portrayed as God's "servant" (to accomplish his purposes for the world).

> But you, Israel, my servant,
>> Jacob, whom I have chosen,
>> the offspring of Abraham, my friend;
> you whom I took from the ends of the earth,
>> and called from its farthest corners,
> saying to you, "You are my servant,

Fig. 5.1 Activity of the Writing Prophets during the Reigns of the Kings of Israel and Judah

Time	King of Judah // Event	Prophet to Judah			Prophet to Israel		King of Israel // Event
780 B.C.							Jeroboam II (783–753)
770							
760	Uzziah				(c. 760)	(c. 760)	
	(Azariah)				Amos	Jonah	
	(767–740)						
						(c. 755)	
						Hosea	Zechariah (753–752)
							Shallum (752)
750	Jotham						Menahem (752–742)
	(750–735)	Micah (c. 742)		Isaiah (c. 740)			Pekahiah (742–740)
740							Pekah (740–732)
	Ahaz (735–715)						Hoshea (752–722)
730							
720							Fall of Samaria (722)
710	Hezekiah (715–686)						
700							
680	Manasseh (686–642)	Nahum (c. 660–630)					
660	Amon (642–640)						
640	Josiah (640–609)	Zephaniah (c. 640–609)					
		Habakkuk (c. 640–609)					
620		(c. 627)					
600		Jeremiah					
	Jehoahaz (609)						
	Jehoiakim (609–597)		(c. 605)				
	Jehoiachin (597)		Daniel				
	Zedekiah (597–586)			(c. 597)			
				Ezekiel			
	Fall of Jerusalem (586)	Obadiah					
		(after 586)					
580							
560							
540							
520	1st return of exiles (538)	Haggai (c. 520)					
	Temple rebuilt (516/515)	Zechariah (c. 520)					
500							
480							
460	2nd return of exiles (458)	Malachi (c. 460)					
440	3rd return of exiles (445)						

Major prophets

Minor prophets

Joel is not displayed as the dates are uncertain and estimates range from the 9th to the 4th centuries B.C.

Micah's prophecy was likely directed toward both Judah and Israel.

I have chosen you and not cast you off";
fear not, for I am with you;
be not dismayed, for I am your God;
I will strengthen you, I will help you,
I will uphold you with my righteous right hand.

It is to the people viewed corporately that God promises, "I will strengthen you, I will help you, I will uphold you" (Isa.

41:10). Similarly, in Isaiah 49:15–16, God addresses "you" (this time feminine singular), a personification of Zion (Isa. 49:14), representing the whole people (see also Isa. 54:1–17).

Awareness of these possibilities should assist the reader in untangling some of the pronoun references that might initially seem difficult to understand.

PART 2

BACKGROUND TO
THE NEW TESTAMENT

6

The Time between the Testaments

J. Julius Scott Jr.

Most of the writers of the New Testament grew up in the world of "Second Temple Judaism," the time between the temple's reconstruction (516 BC) and its final destruction (AD 70). This period introduced changes into the political structure, culture, and religion of the Old Testament world.

Sources of Information

Among the many resources about Second Temple Judaism, the most substantial are the Apocrypha and the pseudepigrapha of the Old Testament, the writings of Josephus (c. AD 37–100), and the writings of the Jewish philosopher Philo (c. 20 BC–AD 50). The 1946–1947 discovery of the Dead Sea Scrolls not only provided new documents from the Second Temple era but also led to different ways of reading and understanding previously known material. The Targums (Aramaic translations and paraphrases of the Bible) and rabbinic literature (which developed over centuries but attained its current written form after the time of the New Testament) also provide some indirect evidence of this period. Because Second Temple Judaism overlaps with the first century, the New Testament itself is a primary source of information about the life, thought, conditions, and situations of that time.

The Apocrypha and Pseudepigrapha

The Apocrypha and pseudepigrapha are collections of Jewish writings from the period of Second Temple Judaism. Most of the fifteen (or fourteen) books of the Apocrypha are included in the canon of the Orthodox and Roman Catholic traditions, and excerpts from them are still read regularly in some Anglican churches.

The word "pseudepigrapha" means "false inscription" or "false title" (referring to the name of the supposed "author" attached to each one). "False" is more a judgment of the names with which the writings are traditionally associated than of their content. Most of these writings represent the beliefs of distinctive groups or schools (or in some cases just individuals) connecting themselves with the name of a notable person of antiquity, such as Enoch, Noah, Moses, or Ezra. Modern collections of the pseudepigrapha contain more than sixty titles.

The Dead Sea Scrolls

Thousands of documents and fragments make up the Dead Sea Scrolls. They contain parts of all Old Testament books except Esther, as well as parts of some apocryphal and pseud-epigraphal writings. "Sectarian documents" are related to the organization, worship, and thought of the group that collected and wrote them.

Fig. 6.1 Major Periods within Second Temple Judaism

Second Temple Judaism developed as political authority changed hands from the
Persians to the Greeks, to the Jewish Hasmoneans, and finally to the Romans.

539–331 BC	331–164 BC	164–63 BC	63 BC–AD 70
The Persian Period	The Hellenistic Period Ptolemaic (Egyptian) Period (320–198) Seleucid (Syrian) Period (198–164)	The Hasmonean (Maccabean) Period	The Roman Period

History

Second Temple Judaism emerged in the fifth century BC during the Persian Empire, which was the dominant power at the end of Old Testament history. The Hebrews, both living in their own land and scattered elsewhere, seem to have had a fairly ordinary existence, apart from events such as rebuilding the temple and the walls of Jerusalem. The book of Esther, however, demonstrates how quickly serious crises could develop for the Jews.

The Hellenistic Period (331–164 BC)

In the 330s BC the Persians were supplanted by the Greeks under Alexander the Great (who ruled 334–323). In addition to military conquest and political control, Alexander was intent to spread Greek (Hellenistic) culture, including use of the Greek language.

The Jews simply shifted allegiance to Alexander and, at first, were generally left alone. Following Alexander's death and the ensuing struggles, his empire was divided among four of his generals.

From 320 to 198 BC, the Jews were controlled by the Egyptian Ptolemaic Empire. A sizable Jewish community also grew in Egypt, and a large Jewish colony in Alexandria was influential well past the time of Christ (e.g., Apollos, Acts 18:24). A Greek translation of the Pentateuch was made in Egypt circa 250 BC, and of the rest of the Old Testament by about 130 BC (together commonly called the Septuagint). Most of Palestine's country-side, outside Jerusalem, adopted Greek culture (Hellenism).

In about 198 BC, the Seleucid (Syrian) Empire to the north of Palestine gained control over the Jews. The Seleucids attempted to spread Hellenism throughout their empire. The Jews were forbidden, on pain of death, to practice their traditional way of life, including their religion. The Jerusalem temple was turned into a pagan shrine, and persecution became prevalent.

Mattathias, an aged priest, along with his five sons, led a revolt. After Mattathias's death, leadership fell to one of his sons, Judas (called "Maccabeus"). Judas and his successors eventually won independence. In 164 BC the temple was cleansed, and the daily burnt offering and other religious ceremonies resumed. The event is still commemorated by Jews each December as Hanukkah, the "Feast of Lights."

The Hasmonean (Maccabean) Period (164–63 BC)

During the Maccabean period (164–63 BC) all rulers were from the same family of Jewish priests (also called the "Hasmonean" family after the Hebrew name of Simon, an early Maccabean leader). Nine rulers followed Judas Maccabeus to the throne, including two of his brothers. From the second generation onward, the Maccabean rulers became progressively dictatorial, corrupt, immoral, and even pagan. Internal strife led Jewish leaders to ask the Roman general Pompey to come and restore order. Pompey did so, but he also brought Roman rule, which began in 63 BC and lasted into the fourth century AD.

The Roman Period (63 BC–AD 135)

When Pompey took Jerusalem, he entered the temple and even the Most Holy Place. To the Jews, this was the ultimate insult and sacrilege. The Romans could not understand why the Jews resented the various exercises of privilege and control by their conqueror. Hence, deep suspicion and ill will began growing, lasting over a century until the Jews rebelled and the Romans destroyed the Jewish state. The New Testament reader must remain aware of this seething undercurrent that colors much of what takes place, even during the ministry of Jesus.

In the centuries before this, Greece had conquered the ancient world and left its intellectual and cultural mark. The Romans built on this through political achievements. Paul and other travelers made good use of the vast system of Roman roads. Roman government, organization, law, money, taxation, culture, religion, army, and demands were everywhere. "Roman Peace" (*Pax Romana*) was enforced by arms but brought a measure of security and stability to the empire. The levels of its society were clearly understood, and the higher levels often oppressed the lowest. In most strata of society, morals were degenerate. Some captured peoples were restless, yearning to be free from Rome—none more than the Jews. Many, like the prophetess Anna, were patiently "waiting for the redemption of Jerusalem" (Luke 2:38).

Roman influence, good and bad, was an ever-present reality in the New Testament world. Zechariah, the father of John the Baptist, prayed for a salvation that combined deliverance "from . . . our enemies" with increased religious fervor, "that we . . . might serve him [the Lord] without fear, in holiness and righteousness" (Luke 1:70–75). One Jewish group, the Zealots, sought violent, armed rebellion for religious reasons. The dominion of the Romans over the land where Jesus lived was most evident through the governmental structures they established, the rulers they appointed, and the actions they carried out. The Jewish Sanhedrin, or Council (a combination civil-religious body), predated the coming of the Romans. It retained broad authority, but always under the watchful eye of Rome. The high priest was the head of these seventy (or seventy-two) officials, but rulers under the Romans removed and appointed high priests at will (in spite of the Old Testament provision that the high priesthood was for life). Tax collectors collected taxes for Rome. They were given, and many used, wide freedom in the amount they collected. The Jews hated them for collaborating with the Romans; they suspected that these tax collectors collected enough to satisfy not only their Roman masters but also their own greed.

In 37 BC the Roman senate appointed Herod the Great to be "king" of all Palestine. Until his death in 4 BC, he maintained this position by cooperating with whatever Roman group or emperor happened to be in power. He was king when Jesus was born (c. 5 BC). It was Herod who killed the boy babies in Bethlehem (Matt. 2:16–18), an unsurprising atrocity, similar in character to his treatment of friends and family.

Herod carried out great building projects. About 20/19 BC he began enlarging and reconstructing the temple in Jerusalem. The main work was completed fairly quickly, but additional improvements continued until AD 64 (see John 2:20).

Herod's will divided his kingdom between three sons. After changing and ratifying Herod's will, Roman authorities made Archelaus the ethnarch (ruler of half a "kingdom") of Judea, Samaria, and Idumea. Mismanagement led to his banishment in AD 6 (see Matt. 2:22). He was succeeded by governors, the best known being Pontius Pilate, who ruled from AD 26 to 36. Pilate was governor during (1) the ministry of Jesus (c. AD 27–30 or 30–33), (2) Pentecost, (3) the earliest days of the church, (4) Stephen's speech and death, and (5) the beginnings of Christian missions.

The second of Herod's sons, Philip, ruled as tetrarch (ruler of a fourth of a "kingdom") over Ituraea and Trachonitis, areas northeast of Galilee (Luke 3:1). At his death (AD 34) his territory was briefly assigned to the governors who also ruled Judea. Agrippa I (Herod the Great's grandson) was given this territory, with the title "king," in AD 37.

The third of Herod the Great's sons, Herod Antipas (often simply called "Herod" or "Herod the tetrarch" in the Gospels and Acts;) was tetrarch of Galilee and Perea from 4 BC until AD 39. While visiting his half brother Herod Philip (not the tetrarch), Antipas became infatuated with Philip's wife, Herodias, daughter of another half brother, Aristobulus, and mother of Philip's daughter Salome (see Mark 6:22–29.). Contrary to Old Testament law (Lev. 18:16; 20:21), Antipas married her. The denunciation of this union precipitated Herodias's anger against John the Baptist and eventually his imprisonment and death (Matt. 14:4; Mark 6:17–19; Luke 3:19–20).

Antipas (at Herodias's request) asked Emperor Gaius to give him the title of "king," the same as that given to Herodias's brother, Agrippa I. Agrippa charged Herod Antipas with plotting insurrection. Antipas, accompanied by Herodias, was exiled to Gaul (modern France) in AD 39. Antipas's former territory was then given to Agrippa.

In AD 41 the former territory of Archelaus was added to that of Agrippa, thus giving him the same title and virtually the same territory that his grandfather (Herod the Great) had held. During his kingship James, the brother of John, was beheaded (Acts 12:2), and Peter was imprisoned but freed by an angel (Acts 12:3–19). Agrippa was struck by an angel and died in Caesarea in AD 44 (Acts 12:23). Roman governors again ruled after this time. In AD 53 Herod Agrippa II (son of Agrippa I) became "king" of Ituraea and Trachonitis. Galilee and Perea were added to his domain in AD 56 or 61.

Two other Roman governors, Felix (AD 52–60) and Festus (60–62), appear in the biblical account. Paul was held prisoner and given judicial hearings by both (Acts 24:10–27; 25:8). While King Agrippa II and his sister Bernice were visiting Festus, Paul was again called on to make a defense (Acts 25:13–26:31). Festus transferred Paul to Rome for trial (Acts 26:32–28:16).

Adjustment after 586 BC

With the Babylonian victory of 586 BC, the Hebrews faced loss of land, monarchy, the city of Jerusalem, and their temple. They lived under the direct control of foreign rulers, without national identity. Bereft of their own rulers, the Jews found their religious system without political support for protection, implementation, or financial backing.

From this date onward, the majority of the Hebrews were scattered throughout the world. This scattering—the Diaspora, or "Dispersion"—presented a continual threat to racial, ethnic, and cultural identity. The latter included problems related to their distinctive religious outlook, including its ceremonial, dietary, and other practices pertaining to ritual purity. Wherever they lived immediately after 586 BC, the Hebrews faced a "theological crisis." Why had the Lord permitted his people to be conquered? Was he still good, loving, caring, and able to protect them?

By the mid-300s BC, the Hebrews had been back in their own land for two centuries. The second temple was functioning. But then the arrival of Hellenism, with the coming of Alexander the Great in 333 BC and the subsequent reign of his successors, intensified the crisis and introduced new threats.

The Old Testament law, the Torah, had established twin foundational pillars for the proper response to the Lord with whom the Hebrews were in covenant relationship. These were (1) the *temple-centered, ceremonial* pillar and (2) the pillar of *observance of ethical and moral instructions.* Before the Babylonian exile in 586 BC, Hebrew religion had been largely temple-centered and ceremonial; it was denounced by the Old Testament prophets when not combined with a proper effect on life and behavior. The prophets insisted on obedience to God and condemned false trust in the temple and abuses of external forms. Unless the people showed the type of repentance that resulted in a godly life and a true relationship with God, the prophets warned that they would experience God's judgment, marked by the loss of their nation and land.

With the captivity of Judah (586 BC) the prophets had been vindicated. The corporate life of the nation was gone, and the temple was in rubble and ashes. Ceremonial worship was all but impossible. Under similar circumstances, most other ancient religions simply disappeared.

After the return from captivity (538 BC) the temple was rebuilt (516) and the priest-led ceremonial worship was reestablished in Jerusalem. But some Hebrews had decided that their religion could survive without it. At the moment, they most needed an inspired message from the Lord, yet the prophets were silent (*1 Macc.* 4:44–46; 9:27; 14:41–42; Josephus, *Against Apion* 1.38–42; Babylonian Talmud, *Sanhedrin* 11a; *Prayer of Azariah* 15; Dead Sea Scrolls, *Rule of the Community* 11). Even so, the Hebrew religion had begun a remarkable adjustment.

Though the Jewish people retained both the ceremonial pillar of their response to God and the moral-ethical pillar as well, the primary emphasis shifted away from the ceremonial to the moral-ethical. But to obey the law, one needed to know its content, which required study. As a result, the center of worship was no longer exclusively the temple with its liturgy but also the place of learning, the assembly, the local synagogue. The major religious leader was no longer only the priest but also the teacher-rabbi. Such adjustments required careful, detailed study. This resulted in new and different forms of interpretation and the birth of traditions, often additional laws, which supposedly expanded and clarified the written Torah. During the New Testament period these additional laws were taught and passed on both orally and in written form (note the frequent mention of "scribes" in the New Testament). Many people regarded these rabbinic traditions as having a divine origin, equal to the laws in the written

Scriptures, but Jesus pronounced them "the tradition of men" (Mark 7:1–23, esp. v. 8).

Divisions grew within the Judaism of the Second Temple era. Some Jews lived in their ancestral land, others did not; some adopted Hellenistic culture, while others clung to the Hebraic one. (Such culturally oriented conflicts are behind the complaint of Acts 6:1.) The new interpretative methods and the additional traditions increasingly became the subject of disagreement. Groups competed for religious prestige and authority, political power, recognition as being wise, wealth, the satisfaction that they were really in the "right," etc. Thus arose numerous parties, denominations, or sects. The best known are the Sadducees, Pharisees, Zealots, and Essenes. (See ch. 8.) Most of their differences resulted from their distinctive traditions. One example of such differences is seen in the tensions between the Sadducees and Pharisees in Acts 23:6–9 and elsewhere.

Most people in the land of Israel belonged to none of these groups, being too busy earning a living and caring for their families. According to Josephus (*Jewish Antiquities* 18.11–17), the Pharisees were the most influential on the general public; the Sadducees came from aristocratic priestly families and were not generally popular. Most ordinary Jews were devoted to their nation and religion, and some (it is hard to know how many) were genuinely devoted to God (such as Zechariah and Elizabeth, Joseph and Mary, Simeon, and Anna; see Luke 1–2). From such as these came most of Jesus's early followers. With contempt, the Jewish leaders regarded them as "this crowd that does not know the law" (John 7:49).

Conclusion

The Jews revolted against the Romans in AD 66. Before the overthrow of the city and temple in AD 70, Jerusalem Christians fled to the Decapolis city of Pella (probably in response to

Jesus's warning and instruction, Matt. 24:15–16; Mark 13:14; Luke 21:20–24; see 19:43). Afterward, Jewish Christian activity during the first century in Jerusalem was limited, but seems to have continued in Galilee.

Roman victory over this Jewish revolt brought "The Time between the Testaments" to its end. The third era of Hebrew history, Rabbinic Judaism, began about AD 90, under Roman rule, and continues to this day.

From the second century on, Jerusalem was a Gentile city, and Christianity became largely a Gentile movement.

7

The Roman Empire and the Greco-Roman World at the Time of the New Testament

David Chapman

The first-century Roman world of the New Testament lay culturally at the intersection of Hellenism (Greek language and culture) and Roman imperial rule. Hence, to understand this world, it is important first to explore the spread of Hellenism and the rise of Roman might.

History

Although the Greeks had settled and conducted commerce throughout the Mediterranean world long before Alexander the Great (356–323 BC), this Macedonian conqueror is most associated with the spread of Hellenistic (i.e., Greek) culture. Alexander, tutored in Greek philosophy and culture by Aristotle,

Fig. 7.1 The Family of Augustus

Augustus	31 BC–AD 14
Tiberius	AD 14–37
Gaius Caligula	AD 37–41
Claudius	AD 41–54
Nero	AD 54–68

inherited the reins of Macedonian and Greek leadership from his father, Philip, in 336 BC. In short order, Alexander marched through Asia Minor, continued south through Syria and Palestine, was welcomed as ruler of Egypt, and conquered the forces of Persia. Alexander was received with awe in many of these lands, which led their inhabitants (esp. members of the various ruling elites) to accelerate their reception of Hellenistic culture—including Greek language, education, and religion.

In 330 BC Alexander received the title of "Great King" of Persia. Yet his short life ended in 323 BC without a clear successor. Eventually a few of Alexander's generals (later termed the *Diadochoi*, meaning "successors") claimed different portions of his former territory, establishing their own dynastic lines—the Ptolemies of Egypt, the Seleucids of Persia (and portions of Asia Minor), and the Antigonids of Macedon.

As it had so frequently before, Judea again lay between the competing powers of Egypt and Mesopotamia. Although first under Ptolemaic control, Judea was absorbed into the Seleucid Empire (198 BC) during the reign of Antiochus III "the Great." The appeal of Hellenism was not lost on the Judeans, and some sought a wholesale adoption of Greek practices through sending their sons to Greek secondary schools. Pro- and anti-Hellenistic factions formed in Judea. Meanwhile, the Seleucid ruler Antiochus IV "Epiphanes," desiring a subservient and financially supportive Judea, decided to force Hellenistic religious practices on the Jewish people. Circumcision was declared illegal, scriptural texts were destroyed, and pagan worship was instituted. In 168/167 BC the Jerusalem temple was despoiled, as prophesied in Daniel (Dan. 11:31; see 9:27; 12:11; *1 Macc.* 1:54); Jesus draws on this image of the "abomination of desolation" in reference to future events (Matt. 24:15–16).

In reaction to the policies of Antiochus IV, the Hasmonean family (also known as the Maccabees) launched an uprising led by Mattathias and his sons (esp. Judas Maccabeus, Jonathan, and Simon). A combination of guerilla warfare and larger geo-politics (esp. Seleucid losses in Asia Minor and internal coups) led to the success of this Jewish rebellion. For several decades Jews regained autonomy over Judea. The Hasmoneans estab-lished their own royal dynasty, with Jonathan also proclaiming himself high priest (152 BC), although he was not of the proper Zadokite lineage. Many of the Jewish factions known during the time of the New Testament (e.g., Pharisees, Essenes, etc.) likely stem from reactions pro and con to the Hasmonean reign.

Meanwhile, in the West, Roman power was growing. Successive wars with Carthage and Macedon left Rome victorious over the western Mediterranean by 146 BC. Roman expansion con-tinued eastward toward Syria. In 63 BC Pompey marched into Jerusalem and entered the temple. Feuding Judean leaders found that the surest way to secure the Judean crown was to align one-self with Rome. Herod the Great, who was not even fully Jewish, befriended Rome and thus captured for himself the kingship of Judea and surrounding territories (37–4 BC; see Matt. 2:1).

However, Roman internal politics were far from stable in the first century BC. The historic rule of the Roman senate was diminishing with Roman military expansion. The senate attempted to play various generals (notably Julius and Pompey) off one another. In 49 BC Julius crossed the Rubicon River beyond his allotted territory, won handily against Pompey, and assumed dictatorial power. A later senatorial revolt led to the assassi-nation of Julius Caesar (44 BC). Quickly a new alliance was formed as Antony and Octavian defeated the senatorial rebels at Philippi (42 BC). Friction arose between these men, and eventually Octavian destroyed the forces of Antony and Cleopatra at Actium (31 BC). By 27 BC Octavian received the title "Augustus," and the lifelong tribuneship was his in 23. The empire had begun. Throughout much of the New Testament period the family of Augustus held the imperial title (see fig. 7.1).

Judean politics after Herod the Great continued in subjection to Rome. Herod's last will was validated by Augustus, leaving Herod Antipas over Galilee and territory to the north (4 BC–AD 39; see Matt. 14:1; Mark 6:14a), Herod Philip over northern Transjordan (4 BC–AD 34; see Luke 3:1), and Archelaus over Judea (4 BC–AD 6; see Matt. 2:22). The Romans, judging the rule of Archelaus to be inadequate, removed him in favor of a string of Roman governors over Judea. The most famous of these governors, Pontius Pilate (who reigned AD 26–36), was much despised for his despotic acts (see Luke 23:1). Favor with Rome allowed Herod's grandson Agrippa I to rule briefly over Judea (AD 41–44; see Acts 12:1; 12:20–25), but his early death again left the governorship of Judea in the hands of Roman procurators. The Jewish historian Josephus graphically depicts the unwise and often heinous acts of this string of procurators.

Eventually anger with Rome spilled over into the Jewish revolt (AD 66–73/74). The Romans could not permit rebellion in any of their territories, let alone in an important commercial trade center such as Palestine. Thus Vespasian and his son Titus (both future emperors) were sent as generals to suppress the rebellion, which they accomplished with precision and cruelty. The destruction of Jerusalem and the Jewish temple (AD 70) transformed Jewish religion forever. Subsequently, there was a suppressed uprising of Diaspora Jews (esp. in Egypt, AD 115–117) during the reign of Trajan. Some Jews hoped for a rebuild of the Jerusalem temple, but the ineffective Second Jewish Revolt in

Judea under Bar Kochba (AD 132–135, during the emperorship of Hadrian) resulted instead both in a ban on Jews entering Jerusalem and in the building of a temple to Zeus on the former Temple Mount.

Amid this history, Jesus Christ launched his ministry in a Galilee governed by a Roman client king, a Judea under Roman procurators, and a Judaism tinged with Hellenism. After his crucifixion by the Romans and his resurrection, his gospel was carried by the apostles directly into the heart of Greek culture and Roman power.

Social Structure, Economics, Politics, and Law

The social structure of the Roman world differed in some important ways from modern life. For example, it is debated whether ancient Rome had a "middle class." Outside the cities, agrarian life largely consisted of either subsistence farming or of great estate farms. Commerce was key to the life of the empire, and the *Pax Romana* ("peace of Rome") largely relied on safe, well-guarded trade routes (both by land and by sea). Cities thrived with commercial enterprise, as well as with artisan, religious, and intellectual life. Public entertainment included theater, musical performance, rhetorical contests, athletics, and gladiatorial combat.

The central Greco-Roman social unit was the family. Marriage was deemed of great importance, even if sexual activity outside of marriage was prevalent (especially on the part of husbands) and divorce was widely practiced. Patriarchal assumptions were strong, with the father possessing control over, and legal responsibility for, the family. Inheritances were normally passed substantially to male children (whether biological or adopted for purposes of inheritance). The role of women varied throughout the empire: some had great autonomy and wealth, while others were cloistered and rarely appeared in public. Children were commonly seen as a blessing, though infanticide and abortion were sometimes practiced. Most households, aside from the poorest, included slaves.

The Roman economy was highly dependent on slavery. Slaves came from conquest in war, voluntary entrance into slavery, or birth into a slave family. There was thus no single racial profile for a slave. The lives of slaves also varied considerably. State-owned slaves who worked in the brutal conditions of the mines had a short life expectancy. Agricultural slaves toiled in the fields. Household slaves served as cooks, hairdressers, servants, and concubines; yet, they could also be trained to positions of significant authority, even administrating businesses for their owners. Such slaves could be granted their freedom, thus achieving the status of "freedmen" and earning the economic benefits of a continued patronage relationship with their former owners. For this reason, some people voluntarily entered into a set period of slavery to wealthy aristocrats.

Patronage relationships were central to economic and political life. The wealthy would agree to be the "patron" of certain "clients," assisting them economically. In return the clients would support their patron by voting for him in his run for political office and by furthering his economic interests. In theory, a chain of patron/client relationships extended from the less prosperous in society all the way up to the emperor, who was the great patron of all Rome.

Citizenship in the New Testament–era empire was gained by birth to citizen parents, emancipation from slavery to citizens, military service, or special edict. Laws generally prescribed less severe punishments for Roman citizens (see Acts 16:37; 22:22–29), and citizens could appeal their legal cases to Rome (see Acts 25:10–12). Despite apparent inequities, a clear legal code, administered through various political officials, is often considered Rome's great contribution to Western society.

Roman government applied a centralized hierarchy of control, while simultaneously granting some freedom of local self-government. Large cities often retained the right to vote for their leaders, who served in economic, religious, and political civic duties. Some regions (such as much of Palestine in the first century) were governed by "client kings," whose monarchical rule was validated by the emperor. The empire was divided into senatorial and imperial provinces, depending upon whether the Roman senate or the emperor appointed the provincial governors. Generally the more outlying (and less militarily secure) provinces were imperial appointments (such as Syria and the regions throughout Palestine), although the emperors also retained control of some important agricultural regions (esp. Egypt).

Education and Philosophy

Most people in antiquity could not afford an extensive education. Slaves were trained for their specific duties; the poor continued in family agrarian life or were apprenticed to a specific craft. However, education was central to the Hellenistic ideal. Formal education was generally private. Certain slaves, called *pedagogues*, could be responsible for overseeing the education of their master's children through hiring teachers (see "guardian" in Gal. 3:24–25). That teacher would educate the children in a set curriculum, including reading and writing, literature, mathematics, Greek and/or Latin, rhetoric, and philosophy. Rhetoric (the study of verbal persuasion) was necessary for political and legal life, and philosophy was considered the highest expression of learning.

Philosophy involved investigation into the physical and conceptual makeup of the world (metaphysics as well as science) and into ethics. Most religions in antiquity did not substantively address ethical matters (Judaism and Christianity were significant exceptions); rather, this was the realm of philosophy. Various competing philosophical systems were taught around the first century (see fig. 7.2).

Fig. 7.2 First-Century Philosophical Systems

Middle Platonists	Expanded and dogmatized upon Plato's concept of the realm of ideas/forms as more substantial than their individual physical expression.
Sophists	Enamored with the successful execution of rhetorical argumentation (sometimes regardless of the particular position taken in the argument).
Cynics	Contended for a more naturalistic way of pious living, often engaging in shocking verbal and physical feats to make their points.
Epicureans	Believed that all that exists were miniscule packets of matter (atoms), that humans were entirely composed of aggregate matter (thus ceasing to exist upon death), and that life was consequently about maximizing earthly pleasure through friendships and enjoyment of life.
Stoics	Argued that the world was fundamentally the expression of a rational force (the *logos*), and that harmonious good living required an exaltation of reason over spontaneous emotions in all of life.

Religion and Magic

Most today think of Roman religion in terms of its pantheon of gods and goddesses, such as Jupiter, Venus, and Mars (or their Greek counterparts Zeus, Aphrodite, and Ares). Certainly, this pantheon was central to civic life. Touring an ancient city, one would see dozens of temples (some of immense size) dedicated to such deities. These gods were thought to act as benefactors both to the individual and to the city. Yet, should one neglect these deities, they could become angry and injure the individual or society. Thus, the charge of "atheism" against early Christians (who refused to worship such gods) was effectively a concern that rejection of civic gods could lead to widespread catastrophe. Ancient pagan worship assumed a kind of ritual contract where, if specific words were said, and if certain sacrifices or libations were performed, the god/goddess was obligated to respond to benefit the worshiper.

Nevertheless, beyond the great gods of the pantheon, each household also worshiped some of the hundreds of other lesser deities that were thought to rule every aspect of human life. Thus Roman houses typically had at their entrance a shrine, a *lararium*, where daily libations were poured to these household gods.

Hero worship in antiquity could lead to the elevation of great conquerors as gods. Thus some revered Alexander the Great as a god in his lifetime. Perhaps it was this tendency that allowed the emperor, as patron of the whole empire, to be received as a god, especially in Asia Minor where extravagant temples to the emperors were built even before the New Testament period. Some emperors (esp. Gaius Caligula, Nero, and Domitian) were known to encourage their own worship.

By the first century AD mystery religions had become widespread throughout the empire, conducting secret ceremonies to gods and goddesses of Asian or Egyptian origin. The inductees learned the mysteries and participated in secretive worship practices.

Magic, though often viewed with suspicion, still played a central role in Roman life (e.g., Acts 13:6; 19:13–20). Alongside the worship of gods of healing (such as Asklepies), magic provided healing remedies, as well as promoting potions, incantations, and charms to provide material and physical blessings or curses. The Romans were also concerned with knowing the future through dreams, prophetic oracles, and various forms of divination (i.e., the reading of portents such as animal entrails, astrological signs, etc.; see Acts 16:16).

Most people in antiquity were involved in syncretistic worship of multiple deities. Yet some were attracted to monotheistic beliefs, especially those of Judaism and Christianity. Judaism had been granted official legitimacy by Rome, and evidences of Diaspora Jewish communities abound throughout the Mediterranean and Mesopotamia. While some admired

Judaism's worship of a single god and its high ethical ideals, others believed its practices (esp. circumcision, Sabbath, and food laws) to be ridiculous. Christianity was often suspected and persecuted for its "atheistic" beliefs (since it rejected all other gods), its worship of a crucified Lord, its practice of the Lord's Supper, and its view of all Christians as "brothers and sisters." Nonetheless, the Christian hope thrived; it was declared a legitimate religion under Constantine in the fourth century and eventually grew to become the dominant faith of people throughout the Roman Empire.

8

Jewish Groups at the Time of the New Testament

John DelHousaye

When Jesus began to proclaim the gospel, the Sadducees, Essenes, and Pharisees were also laying claim to Israel's heritage. Josephus (*Jewish Antiquities* 13.171) mentions the groups for the first time during the high priesthood of Jonathan (152–142 BC) after the demise of the Zadokite priesthood, which had dominated the religious life of Judea for centuries. The Essenes eventually dropped out of public life and became a network of close-knit communities. It is probably for this reason that the New Testament does not mention them. The Sadducees and Pharisees continued to compete for control of the temple and Sanhedrin. By the first century, the Sadducees were dominant (see Acts 5:17). However, the Pharisees remained an influential minority in Jerusalem, and had mounted a successful campaign to win the hearts of the people.

The Sadducees

The Sadducees, including the high priest Caiaphas (AD 18–36), were primarily of wealthy, priestly families in Jerusalem. Josephus claims they were unfriendly—even to one another—and were unpopular (*Jewish War* 2.166; *Jewish Antiquities* 13.298). They could be cruel judges (Josephus, *Jewish Antiquities* 20.199; Mishnah, *Sanhedrin* 7.2; *Makkot* 1.6). When Jesus disrupted their financial interests in the temple, he was arrested and condemned (Mark 11:15–19; 14:53–65). James, the brother of the Lord, was later killed by a Saducean high priest (Josephus, *Jewish Antiquities* 20.200).

The Sadducees rejected the extrabiblical traditions of the Pharisees, perhaps embracing only the Pentateuch as canonical (Josephus, *Jewish Antiquities* 13.297; 18.16). This narrow canon may explain why they did not believe in the general resurrection of the dead (Mark 12:18; Acts 4:1–2; 23:6–8), since it is not explicitly mentioned in the Pentateuch. Perhaps for the same reason, they embraced human responsibility, which is emphasized in the Law of Moses (e.g., Gen. 4:7; Deut. 30:19–20), in contrast to the determinism of the Essenes (Josephus, *Jewish War* 2.164; *Jewish Antiquities* 13.173). Jesus, when arguing for the resurrection (Mark 12:18–27), meets the Sadducees on their own ground by showing the implications of Exodus 3:6 instead of appealing to a more straightforward passage (e.g., Dan. 12:2).

The Essenes

The Essenes lived communally in villages and cities throughout Palestine and Syria (Josephus, *Jewish War* 2.124; 11.1; Philo, *Hypothetica* 11.1). According to Pliny the Elder, an Essene community resided near the Dead Sea (*Natural History* 5.15.73). Some of the Dead Sea Scrolls, which were discovered in caves at Qumran, probably reflect the ideology of this community.

The Essene communities shared all things in common, including food and clothing (Josephus, *Jewish War* 2.122, 127; Philo, *Good Person* 86). Wages were given to a steward, who would purchase and distribute goods to those in need (Josephus, *Jewish War* 2.123; Philo, *Hypothetica* 11.10). They cared for their elderly and sick (Philo, *Good Person* 87). The Jerusalem church adopted a similar way of life (Acts 2:44–45; 4:34–35; James 1:27), except that giving was voluntary (Acts 5:4).

Many of the Essenes did not marry (Josephus, *Jewish War* 2.120; Philo, *Hypothetica* 11.14; Pliny, *Natural History* 5.15.73; but see *Jewish War* 2.160). The group survived by attracting converts. Pliny claims they drew large crowds (*Natural History* 5.15.73). A convert would follow their way of life for a year (Josephus, *Jewish War* 2.137). He could then be baptized, but was not allowed to live with them for another two years (*Jewish War* 2.138). Followers of Jesus were similarly baptized into the church, but without a probationary period (see Acts 2:37–47; 8:37–38).

The Essenes believed God was the cause of all things (Josephus, *Jewish Antiquities* 13.172; 18.18; Philo, *Good Person* 84). Consequently, they viewed all government as divinely ordained (Josephus, *Jewish War* 2.140). However, the Dead Sea Scrolls assume belief in two spirits—one divine, the other satanic—that will be in conflict until the end of the age (e.g., 1QS Col. 3.17–19; Col. 4.16–17). Paul similarly ties spiritual warfare with God's ultimate sovereignty over all things, including government (Rom. 13:1–7; Eph. 2:1–3).

The Essenes were especially scrupulous about maintaining purity. They dressed only in white linen (Josephus, *Jewish War* 2.123). They no longer participated in the sacrifices of the temple, because, in their view, the priests were defiling the sanctuary (Dead Sea Scrolls, *Damascus Document* 5.6–7, 14–15). Josephus claims they offered their own sacrifices (*Jewish Antiquities* 18.19), while Philo assumes they abstained from animal sacrifice altogether (*Good Person* 75). The Dead Sea Scrolls claim prayer is an acceptable sacrifice (Dead Sea Scrolls, *Damascus Document* 11.21; 1QS Col. 9.3–5). They also strictly observed the Sabbath. Whereas Jesus assumes most Jews would pull an ox out of a well on the Sabbath (Luke 14:5), the Dead Sea Scrolls forbid it (*Damascus Document* 11.13).

The Pharisees

The Pharisees resided primarily in Jerusalem (but see Luke 5:17) and were divided into at least three schools: the disciples of Shammai, Hillel, and Gamaliel. These schools were especially concerned about the proper administration of the temple.

The disciples of Shammai, who represented the more conservative wing of the group, were dominant before the destruction of the temple in AD 70 (Mishnah, *Shabbat* 1.4). But Hillel, representing a more liberal interpretation of the Jewish Scriptures, had moved from Babylon to Jerusalem about a generation before Jesus, and gained wide influence as well.

Gamaliel, the son (or grandson) of Hillel, was a renowned teacher of the law in Jerusalem. The apostle Paul had been a disciple of Gamaliel (Acts 22:3). Gamaliel is remembered for his wisdom (Acts 5:34) and careful management of the Jewish calendar. Most Jews followed a lunisolar calendar, which consisted of 12 lunar months, totaling 354 days. Every three years or so a thirteenth month had to be added, in order to bring the average total days of the year up to the 365.25 days of the solar year. Otherwise, the seasons would not have matched the festivals and sacrifices in the temple. Gamaliel determined when to add the thirteenth month (Mishnah, *Rosh Hashshanah* 2.8; *Sanhedrin* 2.6). Ironically, if the Galatian Christians had adopted the calendar of Jewish religious holidays advocated by Paul's opponents (Gal. 4:10), they would have found themselves under the authority of his old teacher!

These three schools attempted to shape the religious life of the ordinary Jew through the dissemination of their traditions (Matt. 23:15; Mark 7:1–13; Josephus, *Jewish Antiquities* 13.297). Galilee was also a part of their mission. The Jerusalem Talmud (*Shabbat* 15d) claims that Johanan ben Zakkai, a disciple of Hillel, spent eighteen years—probably from AD 20 to about 40—teaching in the Galilean town of Araba (or Gabara). So Johanan and Jesus were teaching in Galilee at the same time.

The Pharisees also had considerable influence over local scribes, who would preach in the synagogue according to the Pharisees' interpretations (Matt. 7:29; 23:1–2; Mark 2:16). When the Pharisees in Jerusalem were alerted by some scribes that Jesus was preaching a new teaching with authority, they sent a delegation, which, after observing some alarming behaviors, attributed his miraculous power to Beelzebul (Mark 3:22; 7:1). Since the Pharisees were highly respected by the people, the accusation may have had devastating consequences for Jesus's mission (see Matt. 11:20–24).

The Pharisaic tradition was pragmatic and relevant to the needs of the time. For instance, the Law of Moses requires all loans to be forgiven in the sabbatical (seventh) year (Deut. 15:2). The intention was to provide relief for borrowers, but the reality was that lenders refused to give loans near the seventh year. Hillel addressed the problem by establishing the *prosbol*, a contract that requires a borrower to pay back a lender even in the seventh year (Mishnah, *Shabbat* 7.1). His school was also highly pragmatic when it came to rules for divorce (at least for husbands wanting a divorce), interpreting the ambiguous phrase in Deuteronomy 24:1—"some indecency in her"—as allowing a husband to divorce his wife for almost any reason, including burning his dinner (Mishnah, *Gittin* 9.10). However, the school of Shammai interpreted the law more narrowly, allowing divorce only in the case of adultery.

The Dead Sea Scrolls accuse the Pharisees of being "Seekers of Smooth Things," that is, passing on easy interpretations to the people (e.g., 4Q169 Fragment 1; see Isa. 30:10). While Jesus too was vulnerable to this criticism in some areas of his teaching, especially his indifference to matters of ritual purity and Sabbath observance, he is even more stringent than Moses when it comes to justice. Instead of recommending the *prosbol*, he flatly commands his disciples, "do not refuse the one who would borrow from you" (Matt. 5:42). Concerning divorce, he adopts a similar position to the school of Shammai, but also notes that divorce was not God's original plan and is not required (Matt. 5:31–32; 19:9).

The difference in stringency can be further illustrated by the summations of the law provided by Hillel and Jesus. Hillel says, "What is hateful to you, do not to your neighbor: that is the whole Torah, while the rest is commentary thereof; go and learn it" (Babylonian Talmud, *Shabbat* 31a). Jesus says, "So whatever you wish that others would do to you, do also to them, for this is the Law and the Prophets" (Matt. 7:12). We find the negative wording of Hillel's teaching in earlier Jewish writings (*Tobit* 4:15; Philo, *Hypothetica* 7.6–8). Jesus's summation is more challenging, requiring nothing less than a universal love for all people, including one's enemies (Matt. 5:44).

However, despite the curious quality of some of their tradition, the Pharisees were especially scrupulous to maintain a righteous status before God. Many were probably like Paul, who claimed that as a Pharisee he was "blameless" as to the Law of Moses (Phil. 3:6). While many Jews tithed, Pharisees even tithed their garden herbs (Matt. 23:23). While others fasted periodically, they fasted twice a week (Mark 2:18; Luke 18:12). They also maintained purity at their meals to the point of "straining out a gnat" from a cup (Matt. 23:24; see Mark 7:4), and they avoided sharing a table with "sinners," those like tax collectors who habitually broke the law (Mark 2:16; Luke 7:39).

All three expressions of piety come together in the parable of the Pharisee and the tax collector (Luke 18:9–14). Jesus depicts the Pharisee as distinguishing himself from the tax collector because he fasted and tithed in order to retain a righteous status before God. Elsewhere, Jesus affirms tithing but claims the Pharisees neglect the "weightier matters of the law"—justice, mercy, and faithfulness (Matt. 23:23).

The Pharisees took their personal relationship with God seriously, in part because they believed that the resurrection of the dead was a reward for living a righteous life (Josephus, *Jewish War* 2.163; *Jewish Antiquities* 18.14; Acts 23:8; *Aboth of Rabbi Nathan* 5A). But Jesus says, "For I tell you, unless your righteousness exceeds that of the scribes and Pharisees, you will never enter the kingdom of heaven" (Matt. 5:20). On another occasion, he tells the Pharisaic teacher Nicodemus that he needs to be "born again," or "born from above" (*anōthen*, John 3:3). Despite the blameless way of life many Pharisees pursued, such effort, in Jesus's view, was not enough: like all people, they needed to repent and believe in the gospel. From this perspective, Paul could anticipate being found by God, at the resurrection, "not having a righteousness of my own that comes from the law, but that which comes through faith in Christ" (Phil. 3:9).

PART 3

NEW TESTAMENT

9

The Theology of the New Testament

Thomas R. Schreiner

New Testament theology as a discipline is a branch of what scholars call "biblical theology." Systematic theology and biblical theology overlap considerably, since both explore the theology found in the Bible. Biblical theology, however, concentrates on the historical story line of the Bible and explains the various steps in the progressive outworking of God's plan in redemptive history. In this article some of the main themes of New Testament theology are presented.

Already but Not Yet

The message of the New Testament cannot be separated from that of the Old Testament. The Old Testament promised that God would save his people, beginning with the promise that the seed of the woman would triumph over the seed of the Serpent (Gen. 3:15). God's saving promises were developed especially in the covenants he made with his people: (1) the covenant with Abraham promised God's people land, seed, and universal blessing (Gen. 12:1–3); (2) the Mosaic covenant pledged blessing if Israel obeyed the Lord (Exodus 19–24); (3) the Davidic covenant promised a king in the Davidic line forever, and that through this king the promises originally made to Abraham would become a reality (2 Samuel 7; Psalms 89; 132); and (4) the new covenant promised that God would give his Spirit to his people and write his law on their hearts, so that they would obey his will (Jer. 31:31–34; Ezek. 36:26–27).

As John the Baptist and Jesus arrived on the scene, it was obvious that God's saving promises had not yet been realized. The Romans ruled over Israel, and a Davidic king did not reign in the land. The universal blessing promised to Abraham was scarcely a reality, for even in Israel it was sin, not righteousness, that reigned. John the Baptist therefore summoned the people of Israel to repent and to receive baptism for the forgiveness of their sins, so that they would be prepared for a coming One who would pour out the Spirit and judge the wicked.

Jesus of Nazareth represents the fulfillment of what John the Baptist prophesied. Jesus, like John, announced the imminent arrival of the kingdom of God (Mark 1:15), which is another way of saying that the saving promises found in the Old Testament were about to be realized. The kingdom of God, however, came in a most unexpected way. The Jews had anticipated that when the kingdom arrived, the enemies of God would be immediately wiped out and a new creation would dawn (Isa. 65:17). Jesus taught, however, that the kingdom was present in his person and ministry (Luke 17:20–21)—and yet the foes of the kingdom were not instantly annihilated. The kingdom did not come with apocalyptic power but in a small and almost imperceptible form. It was as small as a mustard seed, and yet it would grow into a great tree that would tower over the entire earth. It was as undetectable as leaven mixed into flour, but the leaven would eventually transform the entire batch of dough (Matt. 13:31–33). In other words, the kingdom was *already* present in Jesus and his ministry, but it was *not yet* present in its entirety. It was "already—but not yet." It was inaugurated but not consummated. Jesus fulfilled the role of the servant of the Lord in Isaiah 53, taking upon himself the sins of his people and suffering death for the forgiveness of their sins. The day of judgment was still to come in the future, even though there would be an interval between God's beginning to fulfill his promises in Jesus (the kingdom inaugurated) and the final realization of his promises (the kingdom consummated). Jesus, who has been reigning since he rose from the dead, will return and sit on his glorious throne and judge between the sheep and the goats (Matt. 25:31–46). Hence, believers pray both for the progressive growth and for the final consummation of the kingdom in the words "your kingdom come" (Matt. 6:10).

The Synoptic Gospels (Matthew, Mark, and Luke) focus on the promise of the kingdom, and John expresses a similar truth with the phrase "eternal life." Eternal life is the life of the age to come, which will be realized when the new creation dawns. Remarkable in John's Gospel is the claim that those who believe in the Son enjoy the life of the coming age *now*. Those who have put their faith in Jesus have *already* passed from death to life (John 5:24–25), for he is the resurrection and the life (John 11:25). Still, John also looks ahead to the day of the final resurrection, when every person will be judged for what he or she has done (John 5:28–29). While the focus in John is on the initial fulfillment of God's saving promises now, the future and final fulfillment is in view as well.

The already-not-yet theme dominates the entire New Testament and functions as a key to grasping the whole story (fig. 9.1). The resurrection of Jesus indicates that the age to come has arrived, that now is the day of salvation. In the same way the gift of the

Holy Spirit represents one of God's end-time promises. New Testament writers joyously proclaim that the promise of the out-pouring of the Holy Spirit has been fulfilled (e.g., Acts 2:16–21; Rom. 8:9–16; Eph. 1:13–14). The last days have come through Jesus Christ (Heb. 1:1–2), through whom we have received God's final and definitive word. Since the resurrection has penetrated history and the Spirit has been given, we might think that salvation history has been completed—but there is still the "not yet." Jesus has been raised from the dead, but believers await the resurrection of their bodies and must battle against sin until the day of redemption (Rom. 8:10–13, 23; 1 Cor. 15:12–28; 1 Pet. 2:11). Jesus reigns on high at the right hand of God, but all things have not yet been subjected to him (Heb. 2:5–9).

Fulfillment through Jesus Christ, the Son of God

The New Testament highlights the fulfillment of God's saving promises, but it particularly stresses that those promises and covenants are realized through his Son, Jesus the Christ.

Who is Jesus? According to the New Testament, he is the new and better Moses, declaring God's word as the sovereign interpreter of the Mosaic law (Matt. 5:17–48; Heb. 3:1–6). Indeed, the Law and the Prophets point to him and find their fulfillment in him. Jesus is the new Joshua who gives final rest to his people (Heb. 3:7–4:13). He is the true wisdom of God, fulfilling and transcending wisdom themes from the Old Testament (Col. 2:1–3). In the Gospels, Jesus is often recognized as a prophet. Indeed, Jesus is the final prophet predicted by Moses (Deut. 18:15; Acts 3:22–23; 7:37). Jesus's miracles, healings, and authority over demons indicate that the promises of the kingdom are fulfilled in him (Matt. 12:28), but his miracles also indicate that he shares God's authority and is himself divine, for only the Creator-Lord can walk on water and calm the sea (Matt. 8:23–27; see Ps. 107:29). Jesus is the Messiah, who brings to realization the promise that

One would sit on David's throne forever. Recognizing Jesus as the Messiah is fundamental to all the Gospels and the missionary preaching of Acts, and is an accepted truth in the Epistles and Revelation.

The stature of Jesus shines out in the New Testament narrative, for he authoritatively calls on others to be his disciples, summoning them to follow him (Matt. 4:18–22; Luke 9:57–62). Indeed, a person's response to Jesus determines his or her final destiny (Matt. 10:32–33; see 1 Cor. 16:22). Jesus is the Son of Man who will receive the kingdom from the Ancient of Days (Dan. 7:13–14) and will reign forever. The Gospels emphasize, however, that his reign has been realized through suffering, for he is also the servant of the Lord who has atoned for the sins of his people (Isa. 52:13–53:12; Mark 14:24; Rom. 4:25; 1 Pet. 2:21–25).

This One who atones for sin is fully God and divine. He has the authority to forgive sins (Mark 2:7). Various New Testament occurrences of the word "name" indicate Jesus's divine status: people prophesy in his name (Matt. 7:22) and are to hope in his name (Matt. 12:21), and salvation comes in his name alone (Acts 4:12). But the Old Testament establishes that human beings are to prophesy only in God's name, hope only in the Lord, and find salvation only in him; thus, such use of Jesus's name indicates his divinity.

The Greek translation of the Old Testament (the Septuagint) identifies Yahweh as "the Lord." In quoting or alluding to Old Testament texts that refer to Yahweh, the New Testament authors often apply the title "Lord" to Jesus and evidently use it in that strong Old Testament sense (e.g., Acts 2:21; Phil. 2:10–11; Heb. 1:10–12). The title is therefore another clear piece of evidence supporting Christ's divinity. Jesus is the image of God (Col. 1:15; see Heb. 1:3), is in the very form of God, and is equal to God, though he temporarily surrendered some of the privileges of deity by being clothed with humanity so that human beings could be saved (Phil. 2:6–8). Jesus as the Son of God enjoys a unique and eternal relationship with God (see Matt. 28:18; John 20:31; Rom. 8:32), and he is worshiped just as the Father is (see Revelation 4–5). His majestic stature is memorialized by a meal celebrated in his memory (Mark 14:22–25) and by people being baptized in his name (Acts 2:38; 10:48). The Son of God is the eternal divine Word (Gk. *Logos*) who has become flesh and has been identified as the man who is God's Son (John 1:1, 14). Finally, in a number of texts Jesus is specifically called "God" (e.g., John 1:1, 18; 20:28; Rom. 9:5; Titus 2:13; Heb. 1:8; 2 Pet. 1:1). Such texts involve no trace of the heresy of either modalism or tritheism. Rather, such statements contain the raw materials from which the doctrine of the Trinity was rightly formulated.

New Testament theology, then, is Christ-centered and God-focused, for what Christ does on earth brings glory to God (John 17:1; Phil. 2:11). The New Testament particularly focuses on Jesus's work on the cross, by which he redeemed and saved his people. The story line in each of the Gospels culminates in and focuses on Jesus's death and resurrection. Indeed, the narrative of Jesus's suffering and death consumes a significant amount of space in the Gospels, indicating that the cross and resurrection are the point of the story. In Acts we see the growth of the church and the expansion of the mission, as the apostles and others proclaim the crucified and resurrected Lord. The Epistles explain the significance of Jesus's work on the cross and his resurrection, so that believers are enabled to grasp the height, depth, breadth, and width of the love of God (Rom. 8:39). The significance of the cross is explained in relation to themes such as new creation, adoption, forgiveness of sins, justification, reconciliation, redemption, sanctification, and propitiation. Woven together, these themes teach that salvation comes from the Lord, and that Jesus as the Christ has redeemed his people from the guilt and bondage of sin.

The Promise of the Holy Spirit

Bound up with the work of Christ is the work of the Holy Spirit. Jesus promised to send the Spirit to those who are truly his disciples (John 14:16–17, 26; 15:26), and he poured out the Spirit on his people at Pentecost (Acts 2:1–4, 33) after he had been exalted to the right hand of the Father. The Spirit was given to bring glory to Jesus Christ (John 16:14), so that Christ would be magnified as the great Savior and Redeemer. Luke and Acts in particular emphasize that the Spirit is given for ministry, so that the church is empowered to bear witness to Jesus Christ. At the same time, having the Spirit within is the mark of a person belonging to the people of God (Acts 10:44–48; 15:7–9; Rom. 8:9; Gal. 3:1–5). The Spirit also strengthens believers, so that they are enabled to live in a way that is pleasing to God. Transformation into Christlikeness is the Spirit's work (Rom. 8:2, 4, 13–14; 2 Cor. 3:18; Gal. 5:16, 18).

The Human Response

Because of sin, all humanity stands in need of the salvation that Christ brings. The power of sin is reflected in the biblical story line, for even Israel as the chosen people of the Lord lived under the dominion of sin, showing that the written law of God by its own power cannot deliver human beings from bondage to sin. Paul emphasizes that sin and death are twin powers that rule over all people, so that they stand in need of the redemption Christ brings (see Rom. 1:18–3:20; 5:1–7:25). Sin does not merely constitute failure to keep the law of God, but represents personal rebellion against God's lordship (1 John 3:4). The essence of sin is idolatry, in which people refuse to give thanks and praise to the one and only God, and worship the creature rather than the Creator (Rom. 1:18–25).

But sin is not the last word, since Jesus Christ came to save sinners, thereby highlighting the mercy and grace of God. The fundamental response demanded by God is faith and repentance (see Acts 2:38). The call to faith and repentance is evident in the ministry of John the Baptist, in Jesus's announcement of the kingdom (Mark 1:15), in the speeches in Acts, in the Pauline letters, and throughout the New Testament. Those who desire to be part of Jesus's new community (the church) and part of the kingdom of God (God's rule in people's hearts and lives) must forsake false gods, renounce self-worship and evil, and turn to Jesus as Lord and Master. The call to repentance is nothing less than a summons to abandonment of sin and to personal faith, whereby people are called to trust in the saving work of the Lord on their behalf instead of thinking that they can save themselves. All people everywhere have violated God's will and must look outside of themselves to the saving work of Christ for deliverance from God's wrath. Indeed, the whole of the New Testament can be understood as a call to repentance and faith (see Hebrews 11). Even those who are already believers are to exert themselves in faith and repentance as long as life lasts, for this is the mark of Christ's true disciples. The New Testament writers constantly encourage their readers to persevere in faith until the end, and warn of the dangers of rejecting Jesus as Lord at any stage. True believers testify that salvation is of the Lord, and that Jesus Christ is the One who has delivered them from the coming wrath.

The People of God

The saving promises of God, then, have begun to be fulfilled in a new community, the church of Jesus Christ. The church is composed of believers in Jesus Christ, both Jews and Gentiles, for the laws in the Old Testament that separated Jews from Gentiles (e.g., circumcision, purity laws, and special festivals and holidays) are no longer in force. The church is God's new temple, indwelt by the Holy Spirit, and is called to live out the beauty of the

Fig. 9.1 The Already and Not Yet of the Last Days

The Old Testament prophets, writing from the vantage point of their present age (the time of promise), spoke of "the last days" as being the time of fulfillment in the distant future (e.g., Jer. 23:20; 49:39; Ezek. 38:16; Hos. 3:5; Mic. 4:1).

The Structure of the OT Expectation of the Last Days

The Present Age
(of the OT writers)   The Last Days

The Time   The Time
of Promise   of Fulfillment

The New Testament (the time of fulfillment), however, locates "the last days" in the present age. The "last days" *already* began with the death and resurrection of Jesus and the outpouring of the Spirit, but they are *not yet* fully realized, which will happen only after Christ returns.

The NT Restructuring of the OT Expection of the Last Days

(Partially Realized)   The Age to Come   (Fully Realized)

The Last Days | Christ Returns

The Present Age
(of the NT authors)

The Time of Promise   The Time
(the time of the OT)   of Fulfillment

gospel by showing the supreme mark of Christ's disciples: love for one another (John 13:34–35).

The church recognizes, however, that she exists in an interim state. She eagerly awaits the return of Jesus Christ, and the consummation of all of God's purposes. In the interim, the church is to live out her life in holiness and godliness as the radiant bride of Christ, and to herald the good news of salvation to the ends of the earth, so that others who live in the darkness of sin may be transferred from Satan's kingdom to the kingdom of the Lord. The church longs for the day when she will behold God face-to-face and worship Jesus Christ forever. The new creation will be a full reality, all things will be new, and the Lord will be praised forever for his love and mercy and grace—for New Testament theology is ultimately about glorifying and praising God.

10

Reading the Gospels and Acts

Darrell Bock

The Gospels and Acts were designed to be read as full accounts, each in their own right, even as they seek to tell about Jesus and his followers. The main obstacle in the Gospels continues into Acts: many in Israel have rejected a message and promise origi- nally intended for them. A key to understanding these accounts is to trace the negative reaction and what it teaches about how people respond to God, and how God still moves to draw people to himself.

Genre

The Gospels have a genre parallel in the ancient world that was called the *bios*. This was ancient biography. Rather than focusing on physical description and tracing psychological thinking and personal development like modern biographies, a *bios* highlighted the key events that surrounded a person and his teaching. That is very much what the Gospels do. The key characters are Jesus and God, as Jesus carries out the plan of the Father.

Acts belongs to a different kind of genre. It is a *legitimization* document: its goal is to explain and legitimate the early church and its roots. This was necessary because in the ancient world what counted in religion was its age and time-tested quality. Since Christianity was new, it needed to explain how it could be new and still be of merit. The answer was that, although the *form* of Christianity was new, the *faith itself* was old, rooted in promises and commitments made to Israel. In fact, the new movement did not seek to make itself into a new entity but was moved in a new direction only when official Judaism rejected it and expelled it from the synagogue, with the result that (in accord with God's plan, as Acts clarifies) the gospel was taken to the Gentiles also. Acts tells this story as it presents how the promise of God expanded as far as Rome.

Though the Gospels are historical writings, they are not always presented in a strict chronology, since some of their scenes are organized topically. For example, Mark 2:1–3:6 reports five controversies in a row that Matthew spreads out over chapters 8–12.

Perspectives

Even though the Gospels each offer varying accounts, they all share the view that Jesus is the promised Messiah, uniquely related to God to bring his promise and salvation. Three of the Gospels (called the Synoptics because they overlap at many places) tell the story of Jesus "from the earth up," gradually depicting how one can see his unique relationship to the Father. Mark starts with John the Baptist, while Matthew and Luke start with Jesus's unique birth. John, however, tells the story very much "from heaven down." He starts with the preincarnate Word becoming flesh. His presentation of Jesus as Son of God is more direct and

119

explicit. The Synoptics allow the reader to gradually see this idea, much in the manner people come to realize gradually who Jesus is. This difference in how the story unfolds does not represent a conflicting account of Jesus, but simply a distinct perspective on how to highlight who he is and what he has done.

Acts chronicles the expansion of Jesus's newly formed community from Jerusalem to Rome. Here God and Jesus are the key figures, directing the action through the Spirit, with the key human figures being Peter, Stephen, Philip, and Paul. Acts is not a defense of Paul, as many argue, but is a defense of what Paul's ministry to the Gentiles represents: the realization of God's promise to reconcile all people groups to himself and to one another through Jesus.

Distinctives of Matthew

Matthew's major concerns include Jesus's relationship to Israel and explaining Israel's rejection of him. Those who were Christians did not seek a break with Judaism but had separated from Judaism because the nation rejected the completion of the divine and scriptural promise Jesus brought and offered. However, that rejection did not stop the arrival of the promise; it raised the stakes of discipleship and led to the creation of a new entity, the church. The message was not limited to Israel but included the whole world. Five discourse units consisting of six discourses (long sections of teaching by Jesus) are the backbone of the book (chs. 5–7; 10; 13; 18; 24–25 [eschatological discourse followed by a parables section]). As with all the Gospels, there is an interaction and interchange between Jesus's word and deeds. Jesus's actions support what he preaches. Jesus's death was an act of the divine plan that led to his vindication and mission. Disciples are those who come to Jesus in personal relationship and trust, seeking forgiveness and the righteousness that God so graciously offers.

A brief listing of major Matthean themes shows the variety of his interests. (Italics identify the key themes, which in some cases overlap with other Gospels and in other cases are unique.) Matthew's Christology presents a *royal, messianic understanding of Jesus*, who as *Son of God* comes to be seen as the revealer of God's will and the bearer of divine authority. As the promised King of the Jews, Jesus heals, teaches *the real meaning of the Old Testament in all its dimensions*, calls for a *practical righteousness*, inaugurates the kingdom, and teaches about the *mystery* elements of God's promise. Matthew associates all of this with a program he calls the *kingdom of heaven*. This kingdom is both present and yet to come (12:28; 13:1–52; 24:1–25:46). Jesus proclaims its hope throughout the nation to the lost sheep of *Israel*. He *calls on them to repent, challenges their current practices, expresses his authority over sin and the Sabbath*, and *calls them to read the law with mercy*. Most of Israel rejects the message, but the mystery is that the promise comes despite that rejection. One day that kingdom will encompass the entire world (see the parables of ch. 13). At the consummation, the authority of Jesus in that kingdom will be evident to all in a *judgment* rendered on the entire creation (chs. 24–25). Thus, for Matthew the kingdom program, eschatology, and salvation history are all bound together.

Distinctives of Mark

Mark is generally regarded today as the first Gospel to have been written, although a minority of scholars regard Matthew as first. Thus, Mark's outline of Jesus's ministry has become the basic structure through which his life has been traced, even though sections of it are probably given in topical rather than chronological arrangement (e.g., the conflicts of chs. 2–3). The first major section of this Gospel (1:16–8:26) cycles through a consistent structure in each of its three parts. There is a story about disciples at the start (1:16–20; 3:13–19; 6:7–13) and a note about rejection or a summary at the end (3:7–12; 6:1–6; 8:22–26). The turning point of the Gospel is the confession in 8:27–31 that Jesus is the Christ. Half of the Gospel treats the movement toward the final week of Jesus's ministry, while a full quarter of it is on the last week alone. For Mark, the events of the final week are central to the story.

The key themes are also evident in how the account proceeds. It begins with a note that what is being told is *the gospel*. Though to a lesser degree than Matthew or Luke, Mark also traces the *kingdom of God* as a theme. For Mark, it has elements that indicate its initial presence, while the bulk of the emphasis is that it will come in fullness one day in the future. The *mystery of the kingdom* is that it starts out small but will accomplish all that God has called it to be. It will grow into a full harvest.

Mark is more a Gospel of *action* than of teaching. Things happen *immediately*, one of Mark's favorite expressions. Mark has only two discourses, the parables of the kingdom (4:1–33) and the eschatological discourse (13:1–37). Miracles abound. Mark has twenty *miracle accounts*. Combined with healing summaries, these units comprise a third of the Gospel and are nearly one-half of the first ten chapters. These pictures of Jesus's authority are important to Mark, as he presents Jesus as one who teaches with authority. The authority underscores that Jesus is *the Christ, the Son of God* (1:1; 8:29; 15:39). Mark's Christology presents Jesus as this promised figure. His claims of authority over sin, human relationships, and practices tied to purity, Sabbath, and temple get him into trouble with the Jewish leaders, who early on determine they must stop him. This *conflict raised by Jesus's claims* is also a central feature of the Gospel.

However, Jesus's authority is not one of raw power. In terms of proportion, Mark highlights Jesus as *the suffering Son of Man and suffering servant* more than the other Gospels. His mission is to come and give his life *as a ransom for many* (10:45). The importance of understanding the suffering role probably explains the *commands for silence* given to those, including demons, who recognize Jesus as Messiah (1:44; 3:11; 5:43; 9:9). Without an appreciation of his suffering, Jesus's messianic calling is not understood. It is here that the pastoral *demands of discipleship* appear as well (10:35–45; see 8:31–38; 9:33–37). Mark is like Matthew here. After the suffering come glory and vindication. The same Son of Man will return one day to render judgment, as the eschatological discourse reveals (Mark 13). The need for discipleship and really listening to Jesus is clear as Mark notes without hesitation *the failures of the disciples*. Their instincts will not take them in the right direction. Instead, they must trust in God and his ways. In addition, Mark notes *the emotions of Jesus and the disciples* more than any of the other Gospels.

Distinctives of Luke

The third Gospel is the longest. It has a mix of teaching, miracles, and parables. Luke gives more parables than any other Gospel. Whereas Matthew presents teaching in discourse blocks, Luke scatters his teaching throughout his Gospel, usually in smaller units. Many key discourses happen in meal scenes (7:36–50; 11:37–52; 14:1–24; 22:1–38; 24:36–49), which recall Greek symposia where "wisdom" is presented.

Key themes center on *God's plan*. Things *"must be"* (Gk. *dei*) in Luke (2:49; 4:43; 9:22; 24:7, 26, 44–47). God has designed a plan to reach and deliver *the poor, the oppressed, and those caught in Satan's oppressive grip* (4:16–18; 11:14–23). The plan reflects a *promise and fulfillment* structure, where key figures express scriptural realization of the plan (7:28; 16:16). The opening infancy section does this through the use of hymns decorated in scriptural language, underscoring the note of *joy* that works through the Gospel. Things also happen with an immediacy, as many texts speak of what is happening *"today"* (2:11; 4:21;

5:26; 19:9; 22:34; 23:43). The gospel marches forward, as is indicated by *the geographic progression* in the story from Galilee to Jerusalem (9:52–19:44).

Jesus appears as the *Messiah-Servant-Lord*. The basic category is messianic (1:31–35; 3:21–22; 4:16–30; 9:18–20), but as the story proceeds it is clear that this role is one of great authority that can be summarized by the image of *the judging Son of Man* or by the concept of *Lord* (5:24; 20:41–44; 21:27; 22:69). All of these connections reflect what Scripture has said about the plan. Jesus also functions as a *prophet* like Moses, a leader-deliverer-prophet who is to be heard (4:20–30; 9:35). Jesus's miracles provide evidence for the inaugurated presence of the *kingdom*. Ultimately the kingdom brings with its deliverance the *defeat of Satan* (11:14–23; 17:20–21). Yet there also is a future to that kingdom, which will see Jesus return to reign over both Israel and the nations, visibly expressing the sovereignty he now claims (ch. 21). Thus Jesus's deliverance looks to the realization of covenantal promises made to Abraham, David, and the nation (1:45–54).

The national leadership is steadfast in its rejection of the message. Nevertheless, the plan proceeds. *Israel* will experience judgment for her unfaithfulness (19:41–44; 21:20–24). Her city will be destroyed as a picture of what final judgment is like and as an assurance that God's program is taking place. Efforts to call Israel to faithfulness continue despite her refusal to embrace God's care and Promised One.

In the meantime, Jesus forms a *new community* (called "the Way" in the book of Acts). This community is made up of those who *turn* to embrace Jesus's message and follow in *faith*. Acts is really the second half of Luke's story, telling how God led the gospel into the heart of the Roman Empire, despite stiff opposition, through the boldness of exemplary witnesses drawing on God's Spirit.

Distinctives of John

The fourth Gospel's account emphasizes Jesus as the Sent One from God, who acts in unity with the Father. John highlights Jesus's uniqueness from the declaration of the incarnation, through a narration of seven signs, to the use of multiple discourse-dialogues. This Gospel's explicit portrayal of Jesus gives it its literary power.

John's themes focus on *Christology*. Unlike the Synoptics, he speaks little of the kingdom. Rather, it is *eternal life* that is the key theme to express what the Synoptics call the kingdom promise. The emphasis in the term "eternal life" is not only the duration of the life (eternal) but also its quality (i.e., *real, unending life*). Thus, to know the Father and Jesus Christ whom the Father sent is eternal life (17:3). This life is available now (5:24–26). Along with the opportunity is also the prospect of judgment for those who refuse it (3:16–21, 36).

The promise is brought by the *Word/Logos* sent from God in the form of human flesh. The *"I Am" sayings* convey various ways in which Jesus represents the way of God. Each image (light of the world, the resurrection and the life, the good shepherd, the bread of life, the vine) specifies some central role that belongs to Jesus. As *Son*, Jesus only does that which the *Father* shows him. It is the *unity with the Father* in mission that John highlights. Jesus is the hoped-for *Messiah*, as well as the *Son of Man* who ascends and descends between earth and heaven. In this role, he will judge (5:27), be lifted up (3:14), and serve in mediating salvation (3:13; 6:27). Even when Jesus is seen as a *prophet*, it is as a *leader*-prophet like Moses (6:14; 7:40).

Seven *signs* dominate the first two-thirds of the Gospel. The response to them covers the range from rejection (12:37–39) to openness (9:25). Interestingly, unlike the Synoptics, there is no casting out of demons in John. He focuses on acts of healing, restoration, and provision. What these signs especially highlight is *Jesus's superiority to Jewish institutions* (1:17; 2:19–21; 7:37–39; 9:38; 10:1–18). Most of the miracles take place in a setting of Jewish celebrations and underscore how Jesus provides what the feasts celebrate. At the end of the Gospel, blessing comes to those who have faith without the need for such signs (20:29).

Jesus is seen as the *revelator* of God. He makes the Father and his way known, functioning as light (1:14–18). Jesus's death shows the love of the Father for his own people and is an example to disciples of how they should love (13:1, 11–17). Jesus's death also serves to gather God's people together (10:1–18) and is a means by which the Son and Father are glorified as life is made available though him (3:14–16).

Also of great importance to John is *the Spirit*, also called the Helper (Gk. *paraklētos*; see John 14:16–18, 26; 15:26; 16:7–14; 20:22), the one Jesus sends after his death, a point Acts also highlights. This encourager-enabler leads the disciples into the truth, empowers them for ministry and mission, and convicts the world of sin, righteousness, and judgment (John 14:25–31; 16:8–11). He is the one who sustains life (4:8–10; 7:37–39).

Distinctives of Acts

Acts teaches that the new community is rooted in old promises. It does this by telling how God directed the inclusion of Gentiles and took the message from Jerusalem to Rome. The central figures in the book are Peter (chs. 1–5; 10–12); evangelists from the Hellenistic believing community, such as Stephen and Philip (chs. 6–8); and Paul (chs. 9; 13–28). Discourses are important to the book, whether they be *missionary speeches* to call people to belief or *defense speeches* where the Christian mission is explained. In the end, the book makes it clear how an originally

Jewish movement came to include Gentiles. The gospel can go to all the world because (1) Jesus is Lord and (2) God directed that the gospel go into all the world. The book ends on a note of triumph as the gospel comes to Rome, even though believers suffered in terms of injustice and physical persecution in an effort to get the gospel there.

11

Reading the Epistles

Thomas R. Schreiner

Introduction and Timeline

Knowing how to read the Epistles is very important, since they make up twenty-one of the twenty-seven books in the New Testament. Paul wrote thirteen of them. Three were written by the apostle John, two by Peter, one each by James and Jude (the brothers of Jesus), and one by the unknown author of Hebrews. Ascertaining the dates of the Epistles, their places of origin, and the recipients is in some instances quite difficult because, unlike modern books, a date is never included, the recipients are not always mentioned, and the place where the letters were written is not stated. In most cases, though, we can be fairly confident of an approximate date, and the recipients are often explicitly named. We suggest for the Epistles the information shown in figure 11.1 (all dates are AD and approximate).

Unity

Most of these letters have three parts: (1) the opening; (2) the body; and (3) the closing. The opening of a letter has four different elements: (1) the sender (e.g., Paul); (2) the recipients (e.g., the Corinthians); (3) the salutation (e.g., "grace and peace to you"); and (4) a prayer (usually a thanksgiving). Not all the letters follow this pattern. The sender is not named in Hebrews, nor are the recipients. The author of 1 John never identifies himself, nor does he specifically address the readers. Indeed, there is no salutation or prayer in Hebrews or 1 John; both launch immediately into the content of the letter.

The body of the letter, which is the longest section in all the letters, does not follow any particular pattern. Here we need to trace out the flow of thought in each letter carefully. The Pauline letters and Hebrews are marked by careful logical progression, while 1 John repeatedly circles back to the same themes and James writes in a style that is reminiscent of wisdom literature such as Proverbs, a collection of shorter teachings on many topics but with no clear overall structure.

The closings in letters vary considerably. Paul often includes travel plans, commendation of coworkers, prayer, prayer requests, greetings, final instructions, an autographed greeting, and a grace benediction.

Although critical scholars have often argued that many of the letters are composites, being stitched together from a variety of different letters, scholars now generally affirm the unity of the letters and have noted their careful structure and the artistry of their unified composition. It is helpful, therefore, to compose a detailed outline as we study the letters, so that as readers we are able to trace the flow of the argument. By doing this we gain a greater understanding of each letter as a whole, since we are prone to read small sections without having a clear map of the entire document. Moreover, having a good understanding of the entirety of the letter assists significantly in interpretation. Often one part of the letter (e.g., the closing) casts light on other parts.

Themes

The Epistles are distinguished from the Gospels in that they are not narrative compositions. In terms of redemptive history, they are written on the other side of the cross and resurrection, so that they typically reflect more deeply on the significance of Christ's death and resurrection than the Gospels do. The implications of the fulfillment of God's promises in Jesus Christ are explored and applied to the readers in the Epistles. These same themes are present in the Gospels, of course, but they are not set forth in the same fullness, since the nature of Jesus's messianic mission often perplexed his disciples during his earthly ministry, and they grasped these realities in their fullness (though still not exhaustively!) only after the cross and resurrection and with the outpouring of the Spirit at Pentecost. The Epistles have played a major role in the formation of doctrine and Christian theology throughout church history precisely because they expound on the great themes of God's saving work on the cross. Because they reflect on and explain the fulfillment of God's promises in light of the Old Testament and the Gospels, it is particularly fruitful to study their use of the Old Testament, Old Testament allusions, and citations of and allusions to Jesus's teachings. By doing this we understand more clearly how epistolary writers understood the fulfillment of God's promises in Christ. We also perceive how they related the Old Testament and the gospel traditions to the churches, and such an understanding assists us in applying not only the Epistles but also the Old Testament and the Gospels to today's world.

Among the major themes in the Epistles are the following: (1) Jesus Christ is the fulfillment of God's promises in redemptive history. He is Messiah, Lord, the Son of God, and the true revelation of God. (2) The new life of believers is a gift of God, anchored in the cross and empowered by the Holy Spirit. (3) Christians experience salvation by faith, and faith expresses itself in a transformed life. The Epistles spend considerable space elaborating on believers' newness of life. (4) Believers belong to the restored Israel, the church of Jesus Christ, which must live out her calling as God's people in a sinful world. (5) In this present evil age believers suffer affliction and persecution, but they look forward with joy to the coming of Jesus Christ and the consummation of their salvation. (6) False teachers dangerously subvert the true gospel of Christ.

The Circumstances behind the Letters

The Epistles are not abstract philosophical or theological essays that explain the salvation accomplished by Jesus Christ. In almost every instance, they are addressed to specific situations facing churches. It is clear in reading Galatians, Colossians, 2 Peter, and Jude that the letters were written because false teaching had infiltrated the churches. Upon reading 1–2 Corinthians, we realize that Paul wrote in response to various problems in the Corinthian church. The letters are crafted to speak to readers as they face everyday life. In his first letter, Peter addresses readers who were suffering discrimination and persecution. Colossians responds to some kind of mystical teaching that promises readers fullness of life apart from, or going beyond, Christ. Philippians hints that the church suffered from some type of dissension and lack of unity. In the two Thessalonian letters, the church was confused about eschatology, and some believers were apparently becoming lax and failing to work hard. While many themes in Paul's thought are set forth in Romans, even that letter does not represent a comprehensive exposition of the gospel, for we do not find in the letter a developed Christological exposition (cf. Phil. 2:6–11; Col. 1:15–20), an explanation of Paul's eschatology (see 1–2 Thessalonians), or an unfolding of a Pauline doctrine of the church (see Ephesians; 1 Timothy; Titus). Ephesians may be a circular letter sent to a number of churches, in which Paul sets forth a more comprehensive understanding of the church, but even Ephesians lacks a complete exposition of all of Paul's theology. We must mine all of Paul's letters to determine his theology—and God, in his providence, has given us all the letters (and, of course, the whole of Scripture) so that we can understand the "whole counsel of God" (Acts 20:27).

In interpreting the Epistles, then, we should try to understand the specific circumstances that the original readers were facing. Upon reading Galatians, for instance, we see readily enough that Paul is responding to opponents who are subverting the gospel. Our understanding of Paul's purpose in writing Galatians is sharpened if we piece together the clues in the letter to reconstruct the views of Paul's opponents. We see that certain outsiders had infiltrated the church and were arguing that the Galatians must submit to circumcision and keep the Old Testament law in order to be saved (see Gal. 1:7; 2:3–5; 3:1–14; 5:2–6, 12; 6:12–13). Paul contends vigorously that no one is saved by works of law but only through faith in Jesus Christ.

As readers of the Epistles today, we face a disadvantage that the first readers did not have, for they knew firsthand the situation that the letter writer addressed. Our knowledge of the circumstances is partial and incomplete. Reading the letters can be like listening to half of a telephone conversation: we hear only the writer's response to the situation in a particular church. Still, we trust that God in his goodness has given us all we need to know in order to interpret the Epistles adequately and to apply them faithfully.

Pseudonymity

Some scholars have argued that the practice of writing a letter in someone else's name ("pseudonymity") was culturally accepted in

New Testament times, and hence they claim that some of the New Testament letters were not written by the purported authors. For example, it is often claimed that Paul did not write 1–2 Timothy and Titus, or that Peter did not write 2 Peter. But the evidence is lacking that pseudonymity was accepted in letters that were considered to be authoritative and inspired. For instance, in 2 Thessalonians 2:2 Paul specifically criticizes those who claim to write in his name, and he concludes the letter with assurance that the writing is authentically his (3:17). The author of the New Testament apocryphal book *Acts of Paul and Thecla* was removed from his post as bishop for writing the book as if it were by Paul, even though he claimed that he had written out of love for Paul (Tertullian, *On Baptism* 17). In the same way, the *Gospel of Peter* was rejected as an authoritative book in AD 180 by Serapion, the bishop of Antioch, because it was not authentic, even though the author claimed that it had been written by Peter. Serapion said, "For our part, brethren, we both receive Peter and the other apostles as Christ, but the writings which falsely bear their names we reject, as men of experience, knowing that such were not handed down to us" (Eusebius, *Ecclesiastical History* 6.12.1–6).

There is no convincing evidence, then, that pseudonymous writings were accepted as authoritative. Indeed, if Peter did not write 2 Peter, then the author is guilty of deceit and dishonesty because he claims to have been an eyewitness of the transfiguration (2 Pet. 1:16–18) and identifies himself as Peter at the beginning of the letter (2 Pet. 1:1). In the same way, the Pastoral Epistles (1–2 Timothy and Titus) all claim to be by Paul and communicate many details from his life, which would be quite deceptive if Paul did not, in fact, write the letters. Some of the authors may have employed a secretary (*amanuensis*) to assist them in writing, which might account for some of the stylistic differences in the letters. Still, each letter would have been carefully dictated and reviewed by the apostolic author.

Fig. 11.1 The Epistles

Book	Author	Date	Recipients	Place of Writing
James	James	40–45	Jewish Christians in or near Palestine	Jerusalem?
Galatians	Paul	48	South Galatian churches	Syrian Antioch
1 Thessalonians	Paul	49–51	Church in Thessalonica	Corinth
2 Thessalonians	Paul	49–51	Church in Thessalonica	Corinth
1 Corinthians	Paul	53–55	Church in Corinth	Ephesus
2 Corinthians	Paul	55–56	Church in Corinth	Macedonia
Romans	Paul	57	Church in Rome	Corinth
Philippians	Paul	62	Church in Philippi	Rome
Colossians	Paul	62	Church in Colossae	Rome
Philemon	Paul	62	Philemon	Rome
Ephesians	Paul	62	Churches in Asia Minor (circular letter?)	Rome
1 Timothy	Paul	62–64	Timothy	Macedonia?
Titus	Paul	62–64	Titus	Nicopolis
1 Peter	Peter	62–63	Churches in Roman provinces in Asia Minor	Rome
2 Peter	Peter	64–67	Churches in Roman provinces in Asia Minor?	Rome
2 Timothy	Paul	64–67	Timothy	Rome
Jude	Jude	Mid–60s	Jewish Christians in Egypt? Asia Minor? Antioch?	Unknown
Hebrews	Unknown	60–70	Jewish Christians in Rome or in or near Palestine	Unknown
1 John	John	85–95	Churches near Ephesus?	Ephesus
2 John	John	85–95	Church or churches near Ephesus	Ephesus
3 John	John	85–95	Gaius	Ephesus

12

Reading Revelation

Dennis Johnson

Genre

The book of Revelation identifies itself both as "apocalypse" (or "revelation," 1:1) and as prophecy (1:3; 22:7, 10, 18, 19; see also 10:11; 22:9).

"Apocalypse" is derived from the Greek noun *apokalypsis*, meaning "revelation, disclosure, unveiling"—that is, the disclosure of unseen heavenly or future realities. Jewish apocalyptic literature flourished in the centuries following the completion of the Old Testament canon, perhaps in part to help the oppressed people of God find purpose in their sufferings and hope for their future in the absence of genuine prophetic words from God. Apocalyptic literature inherited and magnified features appearing in such Old Testament books as Ezekiel, Daniel, and Zechariah. These features include visions that dramatize the prophet's admission to God's heavenly council and that convey meaning through symbolism, promising an end-time intervention of God to reverse present injustices.

Yet Jewish apocalyptic literature of the period between the Old Testament and New Testament differs from Old Testament prophecy in important respects. Apocalyptic authors remained anonymous and attributed their works to prominent figures of the distant past (e.g., Enoch, Abraham, Moses, Baruch, Ezra), using this literary device ("pseudepigraphy") to invest their message with the weight of antiquity and to suggest that those ancients foretold events in the readers' past and present. Whereas Old Testament prophecy was primarily preached orally and only secondarily preserved in writing, apocalyptic works were crafted literary pieces from their inception. Old Testament prophecy not only comforted a righteous remnant but also called faithless Israel to repent and anticipated the gracious ingathering of Gentiles. Apocalyptic literature, on the other hand, divided humanity into two immutable camps: (1) the holy minority who await God's deliverance, and (2) their persecutors, destined for wrath and beyond the reach of redemption. Finally, although Old Testament prophets pointed ahead to the Lord's future coming, they also emphasized his present involvement with his people in their sins and trials; but apocalyptic literature saw the present as so pervaded by corruption that no saving work of God could be expected before his cataclysmic intervention at the end.

Like Jewish apocalyptic literature and some Old Testament prophecy, the Revelation to John is imparted in symbolic visions and conveyed not in oral preaching but in literary form. Unlike extrabiblical apocalyptic authors, however, John writes in his own name, not that of an ancient saint, and he brings a balanced message of comfort, warning, and rebuke. Because Christ's death has already won the decisive victory over evil, Revelation does not share the pessimism of Jewish apocalyptic literature regarding the present age (transient and sin-infected though it is). Rather, Revelation sees believers as conquerors even now through endurance under suffering and fidelity to the testimony of Jesus, through which even their persecutors are called to salvation through repentance and faith.

Revelation therefore stands in the apocalyptic "wing" of authentic, divinely inspired prophecy (emphasizing visionary experience, symbolism, and literary art), along with such New Testament texts as Jesus's Olivet Discourse (Mark 13) and Paul's discussion of the man of lawlessness (2 Thessalonians 2).

Schools of Interpretation

Four approaches for interpreting Revelation have been distinguished by their understanding of the relationship of the visions to one another and the relationship of the visions to the events of history:

1. *Historicism* understands the literary order of the visions, especially in 4:1–20:6, to symbolize the chronological order of successive historical events that span the entire era from the apostolic church to the return of Christ and the new heaven and earth.

Fig. 12.1 Historicist School

Revelation's Visions

Chs. 1–3: Letters to 7 churches	Chs. 4–19: seals, trumpets, witnesses, woman and dragon, beasts, bowls, harlot, Armageddon	20:1–6: millennium	20:7–22:5: dragon destroyed, all in graves rise, white throne judgment, all things new
1st-century churches	Patristic, medieval, Reformation, modern church ages		second coming, general resurrection, last judgment, new heaven and earth

Historical References and Events

2. *Futurism* likewise treats the order of the visions as reflecting the order of particular historical events (with some exceptions).

Futurists, however, typically view the visions of chapters 4–22 as representing events still future to twenty-first-century readers, thus in a *distant* future from the standpoint of John and the churches of Asia. For many futurists, these coming events include a discrete seven-year period of intense tribulation (chs. 6–19), followed by a millennium (20:1–6) in which Christ will rule on earth before the general resurrection and the inauguration of the new heaven and earth (20:7–22:5).

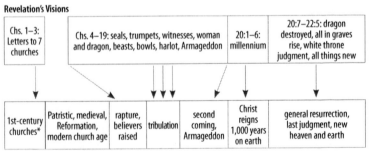

Fig. 12.2 Futurist (Historical Premillennialism)

Revelation's Visions

Chs. 1–3: Letters to 7 churches	Chs. 4–19: seals, trumpets, witnesses, woman and dragon, beasts, bowls, harlot, Armageddon	20:1–6: millennium	20:7–22:5: dragon destroyed, all in graves rise, white throne judgment, all things new

1st-century churches	Patristic, medieval, Reformation, modern church ages	tribulation	second coming, believers raised, Armageddon	Christ reigns 1,000 years on earth	general resurrection, last judgment, new heaven and earth

Historical References and Events

Fig. 12.3 Futurist (Dispensational Premillennialism)

Revelation's Visions

Chs. 1–3: Letters to 7 churches	Chs. 4–19: seals, trumpets, witnesses, woman and dragon, beasts, bowls, harlot, Armageddon	20:1–6: millennium	20:7–22:5: dragon destroyed, all in graves rise, white throne judgment, all things new

1st-century churches*	Patristic, medieval, Reformation, modern church age	rapture, believers raised	tribulation	second coming, Armageddon	Christ reigns 1,000 years on earth	general resurrection, last judgment, new heaven and earth

Historical References and Events

*Some dispensational interpreters think the churches addressed in chs. 2–3 predict different periods in church history.

3. *Preterism* (from Latin *praeteritum*, "the thing that is past") thinks that the fulfillment of most of Revelation's visions already

occurred in the distant past, during the early years of the Christian church. Preterists think these events—either the destruction of Jerusalem or the decline and fall of the Roman Empire, or both— would "soon take place" only from the standpoint of John and the churches of Asia. Some preterists interpret the order of the visions as reflecting the chronological succession of the events they signify, but others recognize the presence of recapitulation (that is, that distinct, successive visions sometimes symbolize the same historical events or forces from complementary perspectives). Full preterism—which insists that *every* prophecy and promise in the New Testament was fulfilled by AD 70—is not a legitimate evangelical option, for it denies Jesus's future bodily return, denies the physical resurrection of believers at the end of history, and denies the physical renewal/re-creation of the present heavens and earth (or their replacement by a "new heaven and earth"). However, preterists who (rightly) insist that these events are still future are called "partial preterists."

Fig. 12.4 Partial Preterist School(s)

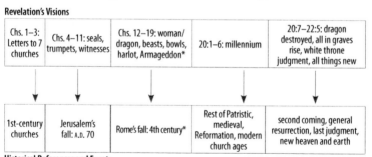

Revelation's Visions

Chs. 1–3: Letters to 7 churches	Chs. 4–11: seals, trumpets, witnesses	Chs. 12–19: woman/ dragon, beasts, bowls, harlot, Armageddon*	20:1–6: millennium	20:7–22:5: dragon destroyed, all in graves rise, white throne judgment, all things new
1st-century churches	Jerusalem's fall: A.D. 70	Rome's fall: 4th century*	Rest of Patristic, medieval, Reformation, modern church ages	second coming, general resurrection, last judgment, new heaven and earth

Historical References and Events

*Partial preterists differ on what would (from the original recipients' viewpoint) precipitate the millennium. This chart represents the view that sees ancient Rome as the church's main enemy. Others would understand Second Temple Judaism as the church's main enemy.

4. *Idealism* agrees with historicism that Revelation's visions symbolize the conflict between Christ and his church on the one hand, and Satan and his evil conspirators on the other, from the

139

apostolic age to Christ's second coming. Yet idealist interpreters believe that the presence of recapitulation means that the visions' literary order need not reflect the temporal order of particular historical events. The forces and conflicts symbolized in Revelation's vision cycles manifest themselves in events that were to occur "soon" from the perspective of the first-century churches (as preterists maintain), but they also find expression in the church's ongoing struggle of persevering faith in the present and foretell a still-future escalation of persecution and divine wrath leading to the return of Christ and the new heaven and earth.

Fig. 12.5 Idealist School

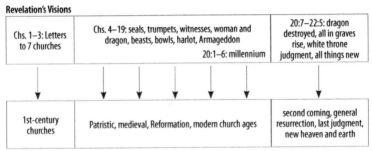

5. Finally, some interpreters hold a *mixed* view, combining features of these various positions, such as saying that many events have both present and future fulfillments, or saying that many events have past fulfillments but that there may still be a future personal Antichrist.

Millennial Views

Christians disagree on the question of whether the Bible generally and the "thousand years" of 20:1–6 specifically predict a future, interim kingdom in which the Lord Jesus will return bodily to earth to reign with resurrected believers during an era of peace, justice, and physical well-being, before history's consummation in the new heaven and earth. Three views have been maintained.

1. *Premillennialism*, usually associated with a *futurist* reading of Revelation, teaches that Christ will return bodily in power and glory *before* (pre-) the "thousand years" (millennium) to defeat and destroy the beast and false prophet in the battle on the "great day of God the Almighty" at Armageddon (16:14–16; 19:11–21). This battle will issue in the binding (but not the destruction) of the devil, preventing him from deceiving the nations for a thousand years (interpreted literally by many premillennialists, but symbolically by others) (20:1–3). During that time Christ's saints, having received their immortal bodies either by resurrection from the dead or by transformation of the living (1 Thess. 4:13–18) in the "first resurrection," will reign with Christ on the present earth, still infected by sin and sorrow but relieved to a significant degree from sin's societal and physical consequences. Although sin, sorrow, and death will not be eliminated until the new heaven and earth displace the first heaven and earth (Rev. 21:1–4; 22:3), the descendants of those who survive the battle of Armageddon will remain on the earth, ruled by resurrected saints, and they will live to extraordinary ages (Isa. 65:20–25). Many premillennialists, especially dispensationalists of various emphases, believe that Old Testament prophecies of Israel's restoration to fidelity and to political and material blessedness will be fulfilled in this millennial kingdom. Although diversity exists among premillennialists regarding the degree to which Revelation's visions and other biblical prophecy should be interpreted "literally" or symbolically, many consider it safer to interpret both the recipients and the content of prophesied blessings as literally as possible, rather than to risk unwarranted symbolism.

At the end of this idyllic foretaste of "paradise restored," a second worldwide rebellion against Jesus's reign will provoke another war, in which the dragon itself will be defeated and finally destroyed. At that point the wicked will be raised bodily to face God's last judgment and eternal wrath in the lake of fire, the "second death" (20:6, 11–14). God will replace the old, curse-infected heaven and earth with the new heaven and earth, where there will be no curse, sin, suffering, sorrow, or death—the eternal home of those whose names are written in the Lamb's book of life (chs. 21–22).

Classical premillennialism expects a future thousand-year reign of Christ on earth (the millennium), with both believers and unbelievers present, prior to the final judgment. Therefore it expects that Christ will come back before (pre-) the millennium. It also expects that believers will go through a time of "great tribulation" before Christ returns.

Pretribulational premillennialism also expects a future thousand-year reign of Christ on earth, but it expects that Christ will first come secretly to take believers from the earth before a "great tribulation" of seven years occurs. After the tribulation, it expects that Christ will come back publicly to reign on the earth, and that he will bring believers back with him at that time.

Fig. 12.6 Classical Premillennialism

(Christ comes before the millennium but *after* the tribulation; the chair, in this and following illustrations, represents the judgment seat of Christ)

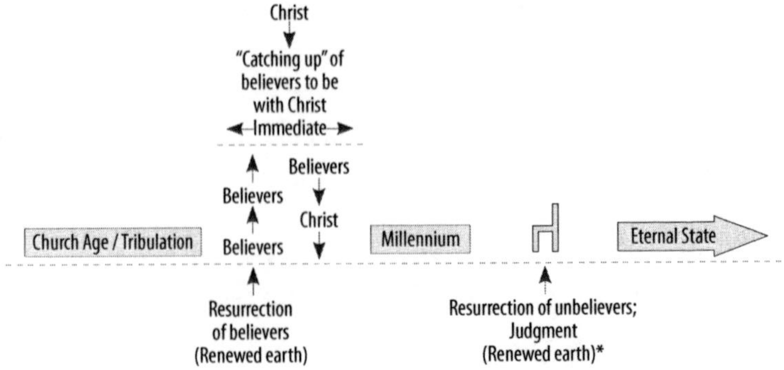

*Classical Premillennialists differ over whether the renewed earth will begin in the millennium or the eternal state.

Fig. 12.7 Pretribulational Premillennialism

(Christ comes before the millennium and *before* the tribulation)

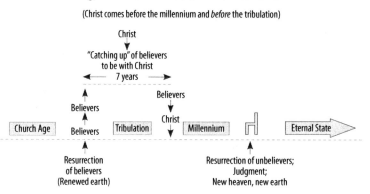

2. *Postmillennialism,* often associated today with *preterism* but also compatible with *historicism,* teaches that Christ will return *after* (post-) the "thousand years" in which the dragon is bound. Classical postmillennialism holds that the "thousand years" is still a future time, a wonderful coming age in which the gospel will triumph so greatly as to thoroughly transform the world's societies and cultures. However, a few postmillennialists think the "thousand years" symbolically portray the historical epoch that began with Christ's ascension and that conditions in this long period will continually improve until they conclude with his glorious second coming. In the postmillennial view, during the millennium Christ is in heaven, not on earth; but he exercises his reign through his Spirit and the church's preaching of the gospel. The "first resurrection" is believers' spiritual transition from death to life through union with the risen Christ (Eph. 2:4–6). Because Satan cannot "deceive the nations any longer" (Rev. 20:3), the church's mission will result in the conversion of all nations and peoples, until the earth is "filled with the knowledge of the glory of the LORD as the waters cover the sea" (Hab. 2:14). This fruit of Jesus's victory will be plain for all to see, as political and legal systems are conformed to God's righteousness, cultural

pursuits such as labor and the arts are redeemed, and increasing quality and length of life are displayed as God's blessing.

After this "millennium," however, for a brief interval before Jesus's return, God will release his restraint on Satan and wicked humanity will converge in a defiant assault on Christ's church. But Jesus will return bodily from heaven in power and glory to defeat and destroy his enemies, to administer the last judgment, and to introduce the new heaven and earth, untainted by sin and its toxic byproducts, in the eternal state.

Fig. 12.8 Postmillennialism

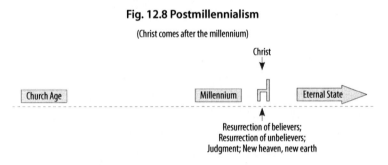

(Christ comes after the millennium)

3. *Amillennialism*, typically advocated by *idealists* but consistent with some expressions of *preterism* or *historicism*, concurs with postmillennialism that Christ will return after the epoch symbolized as "a thousand years" (20:1–6) and that Old Testament prophecies and Revelation's visions are ordinarily to be understood as symbolizing the blessings and trials of the New Testament church, composed of believers in Christ from every nation. However, amillennialists believe that the biblical evidence indicates that there is and will be *no* (a-) millennium in the sense anticipated by premillennialism or postmillennialism before the consummation of history, when sin and curse are utterly banished in the "new heavens and a new earth in which righteousness dwells" (2 Pet. 3:13). Through Christ's death and resurrection Satan was bound, and therefore he is unable to hold the Gentiles in ignorance or gather a world-

wide coalition against the church. Therefore the gospel now advances by the Spirit's power through the church's witness, but always amid opposition and suffering. Just as Jesus the Lamb conquered by being slain, so the victory of his church consists in faithfulness "even unto death" (Rev. 5:9; 12:11). The "first resurrection" is, paradoxically, the martyrs' death, which brings them to heavenly thrones from which they now reign with Christ (20:4–5). The "thousand years" vision prepares the church for a long era of witness and suffering between Christ's first coming to bind Satan (Mark 3:26–27) and his return to destroy Satan. It does not promise relief from persecution, nor a general improvement of living conditions on the sin-infected "first earth," prior to the pristine new heaven and earth. Rather, the vision promises that the dragon, already a defeated foe, cannot thwart God's plan to gather people from all nations into the Lamb's redeemed army.

Invoking recapitulation, amillennialists view Revelation 19:17–21 and 20:9–10 as complementary perspectives on the same last battle at the end of the "thousand years," when Christ will come bodily and gloriously to rescue his suffering church and destroy its enemies: beasts, dragon, their deceived and defiant followers, and—in the general resurrection of the just and the unjust—death itself (20:14; see 1 Cor. 15:26, 54–55). The "appearing of the

Fig. 12.9 Amillennialism

(No future millennium)

Christ

Church Age

Eternal State

Revelation 20:1–6
is now

Resurrection of believers;
Resurrection of unbelievers;
Judgment;
New heaven, new earth

glory of our great God and Savior Jesus Christ" is the "blessed hope" for which believers wait (Titus 2:13).

Each of these three primary millennial views falls within the framework of historic Christian orthodoxy. Though they differ in significant ways with regard to the interpretation of the book of Revelation and other passages related to eschatology, each view is well represented among Bible-believing, orthodox Christians.

PART 4

TIME LINES

Old Testament Time Line

An Overview*

The following dates (all BC) are close approximations based on correlating dates between the Bible and other ancient Near Eastern sources (largely from Assyrian accession lists, Babylonian king lists, or Egyptian historical sources). Often dates can be confirmed between the Assyrian and Babylonian Empires by narratives recording contacts between these two countries.

Patriarchs to Judges (c. 2166–1030)

	1446 Date for Exodus	1260 Date for Exodus
Abraham	2166–1991	2000–1825
Isaac	2066–1886	1900–1720
Jacob	2006–1859	1840–1693
Joseph	1915–1805	1749–1639
Moses's birth	1526	1340
Exodus	1446	1260
Desert wanderings	1446–1406	1260–1220
Entrance into Canaan	1406	1220
Period of the judges	1375 to 1050–1030	1210 to 1050–1030

United Monarchy (c. 1050–931)

	Dates	Notes
Saul's reign	1050–1030 to 1010	Numerals relating to Saul's age and length of reign may be missing in the Hebrew text (see 1 Sam. 13:1)**
David's reign	1010–971	
Solomon's reign	971–931	

Divided Monarchy to Exile (931–586)

Kingdom divided	931	
Syro-Ephraimite war	740–732	Pekah (Israel) and Rezin (Syria) pressure Jotham and Ahaz (Judah) to join their opposition to Tiglath-pileser III (Assyria)
Fall of Samaria (Israel)	722	Shalmaneser V (727–722) and Sargon II (722–705) of Assyria
Josiah's reforms	628	
Battle of Carchemish	605	Daniel and three friends exiled to Babylon
Jerusalem attacked	597	Nebuchadnezzar II takes exiles to Babylon including Jehoiachin and Ezekiel
Fall of Jerusalem (Judah)	586	Nebuchadnezzar II of Babylon

Return from Exile (539–445)

Fall of Babylon	539	Cyrus of Persia (539–530)
1st return of exiles to Jerusalem	538	
Temple building begins	536	
Temple completed	516	Darius I (522–486)
Esther in palace of Xerxes	478	Xerxes I/Ahasuerus (485–464)
2nd return of exiles to Jerusalem under Ezra	458	Artaxerxes I (464–423)
3rd return of exiles to Jerusalem under Nehemiah	445	

*See also Figure 3.1.

**Possible dates for the beginning of Saul's reign are calculated based on other data in the Old Testament: e.g., David's age at accession and length of reign (2 Sam. 5:4–5); Ish-bosheth's age when he became king (2 Sam. 2:10); and Jonathan's probable age in relation to both Ish-bosheth and David, presuming that Jonathan was Saul's firstborn son (1 Sam. 14:49; 31:2) and was at least twenty when referred to as a commander of troops early in Saul's reign (1 Sam. 13:2).

Intertestamental Events Time Line

334–330 BC	Alexander the Great (356–323 BC.) sweeps through Asia Minor and conquers the Persian Empire, including Egypt and Mesopotamia (see Dan. 7:3; 7:6; 8:5; 8:8; 8:20–22; 11:3; cf. 1 Macc. 1:1–7). Alexander imposes the Greek language and culture on all the nations he conquers, marking the beginning of the Hellenistic Age (ranging approximately from the death of Alexander the Great in 323 to the establishment of Roman Imperial rule around 30 BC). As a result of Alexander's imposition of the Greek language on conquered kingdoms, the entire New Testament will later be written in Greek, and will be understandable throughout the ancient world.
333	Alexander the Great passes through Palestine (comprised of Judea and Galilee), extending the influence of Greek thought and culture throughout the region and also into the Judaism of the period. ("Palestine" derives from a Latin name the conquering Romans later gave to this province [c. 63 BC] on the east coast of the Mediterranean Sea, comprising parts of modern Israel, Jordan, and Egypt.)
323–281	In the absence of legitimate heirs, following Alexander the Great's death in 323 BC (cf. 1 Macc. 1:5–9) four of his generals (called the Diadochoi, "successors") divide the conquered territory of his empire into fourths (which then included most of the known world throughout Europe and Asia Minor; see Dan. 7:6; 8:8; 8:20–22; 11:4): (1) Antipater (and later Cassander and then Antigonus I Monophthalmus) ruled in Greece and Macedon; (2) Lysimachus took control in Thrace and much of Asia Minor; (3) Seleucus I Nicator assumed power in Mesopotamia and Persia; and (4) Ptolemy I Lagi Soter became sovereign of Egypt and Palestine.
310*	Zeno of Citium (c. 334–262 BC) founds Stoicism in Athens, a philosophy that prizes logic, reason, and indifference toward pleasure and pain alike. Paul later encounters Stoics and Epicureans in Athens (see Acts 17:18).

307*	Epicurus (c. 341–270 BC) founds the Garden, an egalitarian community based upon friendship, in Athens (see Acts 17:18). The philosophical system of Epicureans stands somewhat opposite Stoicism in its pursuit of pleasure, especially emphasizing the importance of friendships and the luxurious enjoyment of eating, drinking, and other comforts.
277	By 277 BC three Hellenistic kingdoms stabilize out of the four divisions of Alexander the Great's kingdom: (1) the Antigonid dynasty in Macedonia (issuing from Alexander's general Antigonus I Monophthalmus, 382–301, and beginning with his son Demetrius I Poliorcetes in 294/293); (2) the Ptolemaic dynasty in Egypt (issuing from the general Ptolemy I Lagi Soter, 367–283); and (3) the Seleucid dynasty in Syria (issuing from the general Seleucus I Nicator, c. 358–281), the latter which also ruled much of Asia Minor from 312 to 64 (see Dan. 11:4–35). Though Judea will later become controlled by the Seleucids in 198 BC, it is initially under Ptolemaic (Egyptian) rule, with little disturbance.
198	The Seleucids gain control over Judea from the Ptolemies after the battle at Panium (see Dan. 11:15–16). They are led in victory by their king, Antiochus III the Great (reigned 223–187 BC; see Dan. 11:10–19), the father of Antiochus IV Epiphanes (reigned 175–164/163; see Dan. 8:9–10; 8:23; 8:25; 9:24–27; 11:21–38).
190	Antiochus III the Great and the Seleucids are defeated by the Romans at the Battle of Magnesia (fought on the plains of Lydia, in modern Turkey) and forced to pay an indemnity in twelve annual payments. The Seleucids continue to rule over Judea, however.
176*	The Teacher of Righteousness, the founder of the Qumran community (perhaps the Essenes) which produced many of the so-called Dead Sea Scrolls, becomes active.
174	The Seleucid king Antiochus IV Epiphanes (who reigned from 175 to 164/163 BC and was the son of Antiochus III the Great and brother of Seleucus IV Philopator) deposes the Zadokite high priest Onias III (2 Macc. 3:1–4:6), the son of Simon the Just (cf. Sir. 50:1–21). Onias III, who had functioned as the effective head of state for the Jewish people to that time, was replaced with his brother Jason (2 Macc. 4:7–22; see also Dan. 8:9–10). Jason in turn would be supplanted by Menelaus (2 Macc. 4:23–26), who was eventually put to death about 162 BC following a ten-year reign (2 Macc. 13:1–8). ("Zadokite" refers to the descendants of Zadok, a high priest during King David's reign. Zadokites held a monopoly on the Jerusalem priesthood from the time of Solomon forward.) Antiochus IV takes on the name "Epiphanes," meaning "[god] manifest" (cf. 1 Macc. 1:10), however his enemies would call him "Epimanes," meaning "madman."
168/167	Antiochus IV Epiphanes, led into the sanctuary by the high priest Menelaus, loots and desecrates the temple in Jerusalem (1 Macc. 1:20–24; 1:37–64; 2 Macc. 5:11–26; 6:2–5; see also Dan. 11:28–32). On Kislev (Nov.–Dec.) 25, 167 BC (1 Macc. 1:59), an idol devoted to Zeus (Jupiter) was erected in the temple ("the abomination that makes desolate"; see Dan. 11:31; 12:11) and shortly afterward sacrifices (likely swine) were offered up on the altar in the "Most Holy Place."

167/166	Mattathias, father of Judas and his brothers, leads the Maccabean Revolt against Seleucid king Antiochus IV Epiphanes (cf. 1 Macc. 2:1–48; see also Dan. 11:28–35), and dies (1 Macc. 2:49–70).
164	Judas "Maccabeus," third son of Mattathias and second leader of the revolt and later the Jewish government during 166/165–161/160 BC (1 Macc. 3:1–5:68; 6:18–54; 7:26–9:22; cf. 2 Maccabees 8; 10:14–38; 11:1–15; 12; 13:9–22; 14–15) purifies the temple—an event still remembered by Jews at Hanukkah (1 Macc. 4:36–61; see also Dan. 8:12–14; 9:24).
161*	The Zadokite priest Onias IV migrates to Egypt and founds a rival temple at Leontopolis.
152	Jonathan (assumed leadership during 160–143/142 BC; cf. 1 Maccabees 9–12), brother of Judas Maccabeus, fifth son of Mattathias, and third leader of the revolt, accepts the high priesthood as a gift from Alexander Epiphanes (Balas) (1 Macc. 10:1–21), the son of Antiochus IV Epiphanes and pretender to the Seleucid throne. Three distinct sects within Judaism become active at this time: the Essenes (or perhaps Qumran community—the sect with which the Dead Sea Scrolls are most closely connected), the Pharisees, and the Sadducees (see Matt. 3:7). See also ch. 8, "Jewish Groups at the Time of the New Testament."
142	Jewish independence is recognized by Seleucid king Demetrius II Nicator (d. 125 BC; cf. 1 Macc. 13:31–42). Simon, brother of Judas Maccabeus and second son of Mattathias, is named "high priest and commander and leader" of the Judeans (1 Macc. 13:42; cf. 14:35, 41), effectively establishing the Hasmonean Dynasty. Simon rules 142–135 BC (cf. 1 Maccabees 13–16). ("Hasmonean" is derived from the name of Hashman [see Josephus, Jewish Antiquities 12.265], great-grandfather of Mattathias.)
135/134–104	John Hyrcanus I, son of Simon, rules following his father's murder (cf. 1 Macc. 16:11–24).
113	The Hasmonean king John Hyrcanus I destroys the Samaritan temple.
104–103	Judah Aristobulus I, oldest son of John Hyrcanus I, rules.
103–76	Alexander Jannaeus, youngest son of John Hyrcanus I, rules.
88	The Seleucid king Demetrius III Eukairos (son of Antiochus VIII Grypus) is invited by the opponents of Alexander Jannaeus to invade Palestine.
76–67	Salome Alexandra, wife of Alexander Jannaeus, rules.
73–71	Spartacus, a gladiator-slave, leads an ultimately unsuccessful slave revolt (known as the Third Servile War) against the Roman Republic.
67	Civil war breaks out in Judea between supporters of Hyrcanus II and Aristobulus II, Hasmonean brothers. Aristobulus II, older son of Alexander Jannaeus, rules from 67 to 63 BC. Hyrcanus II, younger son of Alexander Jannaeus, rules from 63 to 40 BC. Herod the Great would eventually marry into the Hasmonean Dynasty through his union with the granddaughter of Aristobulus II, Mariamne I.

64	Syria becomes a Roman province, effectively establishing Roman rule on Palestine's northern boundaries.
63	Aemelius Scaurus leads Pompey's armies into Palestine, leading to Roman control over Palestine and thus marking the definitive end of Jewish political independence.
47	The Library of Alexandria is burned. Once the largest library in the world, probably containing half a million scrolls or volumes, it suffers the loss of many primary sources of ancient Greek literary texts, as well as translations or adaptations of important works written in other languages. According to the *Letter of Aristeas*, the Greek translation of the Old Testament called the Septuagint (LXX) was begun for the needs of this library. No works housed in this once great library survived antiquity.
44 (March 15)	Julius Caesar is murdered.
43–40	Parthian invasion and interregnum: Phasael, Herod's brother and tetrarch of Judea ("tetrarch" is a ruler of one of four divisions of a Roman country or province), is killed when the last Hasmonean, Antigonus, the son of Aristobulus II and nephew of Hyrcanus II, gains the support of the Parthians to the east and invades Judea.
40–37	Mattathias Antigonus, son of Aristobulus II, rules from Jerusalem.
40	The Roman Senate declares Herod the Great "King of the Jews," giving him vassal rulership over Palestine (comprised of the provinces Judea and Galilee). His rule does not truly begin until 37 BC, however, when he is able to recapture Jerusalem from Antigonus.
37–4	Herod the Great rules from 37 to 4 BC and is the "legitimate" successor to the Hasmonean Dynasty through his marriage to Mariamne I, granddaughter of both Aristobulus II and Hyrcanus II (her parents were first cousins). Herod recaptures Jerusalem from Antigonus and the Parthians in 37 BC through the help of Roman forces, to whom he had fled for help three years earlier.
37–31	Herod the Great fortifies Masada, a mountaintop fortress in southeast Israel on the southwest shore of the Dead Sea, as a refuge in case of revolt. (Masada would be the site of the last stand of the Zealot Jewish community against the Romans during the revolt of AD. 66–73. After a two-year siege, the Zealots chose to commit mass suicide rather than surrender to the Romans.)
31	Octavian (later called Caesar Augustus) defeats Antony and Cleopatra in the Battle of Actium, effectively consolidating his *de facto* power as the sole ruler of the Roman Empire. His reign lasted until his death in AD 14, with Tiberius assuming power after him.
30	Egypt becomes a Roman province.
20/19	Herod the Great begins rebuilding the temple proper in Jerusalem.

5*	Jesus of Nazareth is born within the province of Judea in the town of Bethlehem during the final years of the reign of Herod the Great (see Matt. 2:1; Luke 1:5–7; 2:2).
4	Herod the Great dies, and his kingdom is divided between his three surviving sons: (1) Herod Archelaus ("Herod the Ethnarch") became ethnarch of Judea, Samaria, and Idumea (or Edom; ruled 4 BC–AD 6; "ethnarch" refers to ruler of a people under the Roman Empire); (2) Herod Antipas became tetrarch of Galilee and Perea (ruled 4 BC–AD 39); and (3) Herod Philip II became tetrarch of Iturea and Trachonitis (ruled 4 BC–AD 34).

* denotes approximate date; / signifies either/or

New Testament Time Line

5 BC*	Jesus is born in Bethlehem.
4 BC	Jesus's family flees to Egypt to escape from Herod's plan to kill Jesus (Matt. 2:13–18); Herod dies; Judas (of Sepphoris) and others rebel, requiring the Syrian Governor Varus to intervene throughout Palestine; Sepphoris, a city four miles from Nazareth, is destroyed by Roman soldiers; Judea, Samaria, and Idumea are given to Herod's son, Archelaus; Galilee and Perea are given to his son Antipas; Jesus's family, after returning from Egypt, resides in Nazareth (Matt. 2:19–23), a small village in southern Galilee.
AD 6	Archelaus is exiled for incompetence; Judea becomes a Roman province; Judas the Galilean (of Gamla) leads a revolt against the tax census; the governor of Syria, Quirinius (AD 6–7), appoints Annas high priest (6–15).
8*	Jesus (age 12) interacts with the teachers in the temple (Luke 2:41–50).
8*–28/30	Jesus works as a carpenter in Nazareth (Matt. 13:55; Mark 6:3) and probably in neighboring villages and Sepphoris, which was being rebuilt.
28–29*	John the Baptist begins his ministry around the Jordan River (John 1:19).
28–30*	Jesus begins his ministry in Judea, but soon focuses his efforts in Galilee. In Jerusalem, Pharisees (like Gamaliel) train disciples (like Paul) in their tradition. They send a delegation to Galilee, but the delegation rejects Jesus's teaching. In Alexandria, Philo (20 BC–AD 50) attempts to unify Greek philosophy with Hebrew Scripture.
33 (or 30)	Jesus returns to Judea, is crucified, and resurrected. James the brother of Jesus becomes a believer after witnessing the resurrected Jesus (1 Cor. 15:7; Acts 12:17). Jesus ascends to the Father's right hand (Acts 1). Jesus's first followers receive the Holy Spirit at Pentecost and begin to proclaim the gospel (Acts 2).

33/34*	Paul witnesses the resurrected Lord on the way to Damascus and is commissioned as an apostle to the nations (Acts 9; Gal. 1:15–16).
34–37	Paul ministers in Damascus and Arabia (Acts 9:19–22; 26:20; Gal. 1:16–18).
36	Pilate loses his position for incompetence.
36/37*	Paul meets with Peter in Jerusalem (Acts 9:26–30; Gal. 1:18).
37–45	Paul ministers in Syria, Tarsus, and Cilicia (Acts 9:30; Gal. 1:21).
38*	Peter witnesses to Cornelius (Acts 10).
39	Antipas is exiled.
40–45*	James writes his letter to believers outside Palestine (see James 1:1).
41–44	Agrippa, Herod the Great's grandson, rules Palestine; he kills James the brother of John (Acts 12:2) and imprisons Peter (Acts 12:3).
42–44	Paul receives his "thorn in the flesh" (2 Cor. 12:7).
44	Peter leaves Jerusalem; Agrippa is killed by an "angel of the Lord" (Acts 12:23).
44–46	Theudas persuades many Jews to sell their possessions and follow him into the wilderness where he claimed he would miraculously divide the Jordan River; Roman procurator Fadus dispatches his cavalry and beheads the would-be messiah.
44–47*	Paul's Second Visit to Jerusalem; time of famine (Acts 11:27–30; Gal. 2:1–10).
46–47	Paul's First Missionary Journey (with Barnabas) from Antioch to Cyprus, Antioch in Pisidia, Iconium, and Lystra (Acts 13:4–14:26).
46–48	Roman procurator Tiberius Alexander crucifies two sons (Jacob and Simon) of Judas the Galilean.
48*	Paul writes *Galatians*, perhaps from Antioch (see Acts 14:26–28).
48–49*	Paul and Peter return to Jerusalem for the Apostolic Council, which, with the assistance of James, frees Gentile believers from the requirement of circumcision in opposition to Pharisaic believers (Acts 15:1–29); Paul and Barnabas return to Antioch (Acts 15:30) but split over a dispute about John Mark (Acts 15:36–40).
48/49–51*	Paul's Second Missionary Journey (with Silas) from Antioch to Syria, Cilicia, southern Galatia, Macedonia, notably Philippi, Thessalonica, and Berea; and then on to Achaia, notably Athens and Corinth (Acts 15:36–18:22).
49	Claudius expels Jews from Rome because of conflicts about Jesus (Acts 18:2); Paul befriends two refugees, Priscilla and Aquila, in Corinth (Acts 18:2–3).
49–51*	Paul writes 1–2 *Thessalonians* from Corinth (Acts 18:1, 11; also see Acts 18:5 with 1 Thess. 1:8).
51	Paul appears before Gallio, proconsul of Achaia (Acts 18:12–17).
50–54*	Peter comes to Rome.

52–57*	Paul's Third Missionary Journey from Antioch to Galatia, Phrygia, Ephesus, Macedonia, Greece (Acts 18:23–21:17).
52–55	Paul ministers in Ephesus (Acts 19:1–20).
53–55*	Mark writes his Gospel, containing Peter's memories of Jesus; perhaps within a decade, Matthew publishes his Gospel, which relies on Mark and other sources. Paul writes 1 Corinthians from Ephesus (Acts 19:10).
54	Claudius dies (edict exiling Jews repealed); Priscilla and Aquila return to Rome and host a church in their home (see Rom. 16:3–5).
54–68	Nero reigns.
55–56*	Paul writes 2 Corinthians from Macedonia (Acts 20:1, 3; 2 Cor. 1:16; 2:13; 7:5; 8:1; 9:2, 4; see 1 Cor. 16:5).
57*	Paul winters in Corinth and writes Romans (Acts 20:3; see Rom. 16:1–2; also see Rom. 16:23 with 1 Cor. 1:14); travels to Jerusalem (Acts 21:1–16), visits with James the brother of Jesus (Acts 21:17–26), and is arrested (Acts 21:27–36; 22:22–29).
57–59	Paul is imprisoned and transferred to Caesarea (Acts 23:23–24, 33–34).
60	Paul begins voyage to Rome (Acts 27:1–2); he is shipwrecked for three months on the island of Malta (Acts 27:39–28:10).
60–70*	Letter to the Hebrews is written.
62	James the brother of the Lord is executed by the Sadducean high priest Ananus.
62–63*	Peter writes his first letter (1 Peter) from Rome (1 Pet. 5:13).
62*	Paul arrives in Rome and remains under house arrest (Acts 28:16–31); he writes Ephesians (see verses for Colossians), Philippians (Phil. 1:7, 13, 17; 4:22), Colossians (Col. 4:3, 10, 18; cf. Acts 27:2 with Col. 4:10), Philemon (see Philem. 23 with Col. 1:7; Philem. 2 with Col. 4:17; Philem. 24 with Col. 4:10; also see Col. 4:9). Luke, Paul's physician and companion (see Col. 4:14), writes Luke and Acts.
62–64	Paul is released, extends his mission (probably reaching Spain), writes 1 Timothy from Macedonia (cf. 1 Tim. 1:3) and Titus from Nicopolis (Titus 3:12); he is rearrested in Rome (2 Tim. 1:16–17).
63–64	Work on the temple complex is completed.
64 (July 19)	Fire in Rome; Nero blames and kills many Christians.
64–67*	Peter writes his second letter (2 Peter). Jude writes his letter. Paul writes 2 Timothy (see 2 Tim. 4:6–8). Paul and Peter are martyred in Rome.
66	First Jewish-Roman War begins with a riot between Greeks and Jews at Caesarea; Roman procurator Gesius Florus (AD 64–66) is murdered and a Roman garrison wiped out; Menahem, son or grandson of Judas the Galilean, murders the high priest Ananias and seizes control of the temple; Nero dispatches Vespasian with three legions.

67*	Romans destroy the Qumran community, who beforehand hid the so-called Dead Sea Scrolls in nearby caves; the church in Jerusalem flees to Pella (Matt. 24:15–16; Mark 13:14; Luke 21:20–22); John migrates to Ephesus with Mary, Jesus's mother.
68	Nero commits suicide; year of the three emperors.
69	Rebellion quelled in Galilee and Samaria; Vespasian summoned back to Rome to become emperor.
70 (Aug. 30)	Titus, Vespasian's son, after a five-month siege of Jerusalem, destroys the temple after desecrating it; the temple's menorah, Torah, and veil are removed and later put on display in a victory parade in Rome; the influence of the Sadducees ends; the Pharisee Johanan ben Zakkai escapes and convinces the Romans to allow him and others to settle in Jamnia, where they found a school.
73 (May 2)*	Before Roman general Silva breaches the fortress atop Masada following a two-year siege, 936 Jewish rebels commit suicide.
75	Titus has an affair with the Jewish princess Bernice, sister of Agrippa II (Acts 25:13, 23), whom he later abandons because of the scandal.
77	Pliny the Elder writes *Natural History*.
77–78	Josephus publishes *Jewish War* in Rome.
79	Pompeii and Herculaneum are destroyed by eruption of Vesuvias; Pliny the Elder dies attempting to investigate.
81	The Arch of Titus, celebrating his destruction of the temple, is erected in Rome.
81–96	Domitian, Titus's brother, persecutes Christians among the Roman nobility, including his own relatives Clemens and Domitilla.
85–95*	John writes his letters (*1–3 John*), probably in Ephesus.
89–95*	John writes his Gospel, probably in Ephesus.
93–94	Josephus publishes *Jewish Antiquities* in Rome.
94	Domitian exiles philosophers from Rome.
95*	Amidst persecution, Clement, a leader in the Roman church, writes his *Letter to the Corinthians* (*1 Clement*) appealing for peace between the young men and elders.
95–96*	Exiled by Domitian to Patmos, John writes *Revelation* (Rev. 1:9).
96–98	Nerva, the first of five "good" emperors, ends official persecution.

* denotes approximate date; / signifies either/or